GLOBETROTTER
TRAVEL GUIDES

ZIMBABWE

PAUL TINGAY

NEW
HOLLAND

GLOBETROTTER
TRAVEL GUIDES

First edition published in 1994 by
New Holland (Publishers) Ltd
London • Cape Town • Sydney

Copyright © 1994 in text: Paul Tingay
Copyright © 1994 in maps: Globetrotter
Travel Maps
Copyright © 1994 in photographs: Individual photographers as credited below.
Copyright © 1994 New Holland (Publishers) Ltd

ISBN 1 85368 366 3

New Holland (Publishers) Ltd
37 Connaught Street, London W2 2AZ

Editor: Mariëlle Renssen
Proofreader: Tessa Kennedy
Indexer: Sandie Vahl
Design concept: Neville Poulter
Design and DTP: Mandy Moss
Cartography: Globetrotter Travel Maps
Reproduction by Hirt & Carter (Pty) Ltd, Cape Town
Printed and bound in Singapore by Tien Wah Press (Pte) Ltd

Although every effort has been made to ensure accuracy of facts, and telephone and fax numbers in this book, the publishers will not be held responsible for changes that occur at the time of going to press.

Photographic credits: **Anthony Bannister/ABPL,** pages 21 (bottom right), 46, 109; **Daryl Balfour,** pages 7, 43, 79, 108, 112, 118; **David Bristow/Photo Access,** pages 8, 47, 119; **Daphne Carew/ABPL,** page 48; **Mike Coppinger,** pages 6, 67 (top), 75 [ABPL]; **Gerald Cubitt,** cover (top left and bottom left), title page, pages 12, 13, 26, 34, 40, 50, 54, 64, 66, 82, 88, 90, 99, 104, 110, 115; **Roger de la Harpe,** cover (top right), pages 14, 53, 55 [ABPL], 60, 78 [ABPL]; **Nigel Dennis,** page 37; **Nic Good,** page 56; **Inpra,** pages 17 [Sygma Press], 19; **Beverly Joubert/ABPL,** page 24; **National Archives of Zimbabwe,** pages 15, 16; **Jackie Nel/Photo Access,** pages 63, 85, 91; **Brendan Ryan/ABPL,** pages 11, 23; **Lorna Stanton,** page 36; **Peter Steyn,** pages 67 (bottom), 80 [Photo Access], 86 [Photo Access]; **Struik Image Library,** pages 28, 76 [Leonard Hoffman], 117 [Peter Pickford]; **Jan Teede,** pages 22, 27, 57, 68, 69, 101, 102; **Paul Tingay,** page 35; **Mark van Aardt,** cover (bottom right), pages 21 (bottom left), 77, 92, 93, 96; **Franz von Hörsten,** pages 72, 87; **Friedrich von Hörsten,** pages 45, 107; **Patrick Wagner/Photo Access,** pages 4, 29, 30; **B&L Worsley/Photo Access,** pages 65, 100.

CONTENTS

1
Introducing Zimbabwe

Zimbabwe, land of the thunderous **Victoria Falls** and the ruins of **Great Zimbabwe**, is heir to an unparalleled wilderness estate: **Gonarezhou**, **Hwange**, the **Zambezi River** and **Matusadona**.

The country is coming to realize, however, that there must be a reconciliation between the economic needs of its fast expanding population of 11 million people and man's spiritual need for the wilderness. Now, rural communities countrywide are being encouraged to manage their own wildlife, and reap the financial benefit. Together with new conservancy projects whereby huge cattle ranches and farms are amalgamating and turning to game and tourism with the active involvement of adjacent communities, this could one day double their wildlife heritage in a shared camp-fire of survival.

Zimbabwe has its cities – the capital **Harare**, Bulawayo, Gwero, Mutare – and there is urban sprawl. But 70% of Zimbabweans still live on small farms, growing their own maize and selling their tobacco, with perhaps the family head or first-born son working in the city to pay for school fees and fertilizer.

Zimbabwe's real beauty lies at its fringes: the Zambezi River valley with its riverine forests and hippo, Lake Kariba with fighting tigerfish and island safari lodges, and Hwange, supporting the world's greatest concentration of elephant. In the southwest is the **Matobo**, land of a thousand hills and kamikaze black eagles, while in the east on the mountainous border with Mozambique, are the trout streams and downs of the **Eastern Highlands**.

TOP ATTRACTIONS

*** **Lake Kariba**: houseboating, tigerfishing, game-viewing by canoe
*** **Victoria Falls**: awesome thundering waters
*** **Mana Pools**: prolific hippo population, walking trails in the wild
*** **Hwange National Park**: renowned for its elephant
** **Great Zimbabwe**: a World Heritage Site, largest ruins complex in Africa
** **Eastern Highlands**: good trout fishing, bracing walks in the rugged mountains.

Opposite: *White-water rafting on the Zambezi River below Victoria Falls.*

THE LAND

Rudyard Kipling's 'great, grey-green greasy Limpopo' forms Zimbabwe's southern border with South Africa, while 650km (404 miles) to the north is the Zambezi (the fourth largest of Africa's rivers after the Nile, Congo and Niger). The land climbs gradually from the hot parklands of these two river valleys, with their big game populations, up through small cattle-plough farms to a central plateau of msasa and mopane savanna-woodland which covers a quarter of the country. It is on this fertile, well-watered ridge – the country's granary – that the main towns are sited.

The central watershed is a fantasy garden of balancing rocks that tower above the surrounding woodlands and open grass plains. These in turn are interspersed with huge whale-back *dwalas* – granite domes the colour of kudu hides – down which the water pours during the rains.

There are three sets of mountains delineating the central ridge: the **Mvurwi** range in the tobacco-growing north, the **Matobo Hills** in the southwest, with the **Mashava Hills** in the centre, near Ngezi Recreational Park and the town of Kwekwe.

Right: *The Zambezi's spectacular Batoka gorge is spanned by Cecil John Rhodes' famed railway bridge linking Zimbabwe with Zambia.* **Opposite:** *The heat-hazed landscape of Gonarezhou National Park; the region is noted for its giant baobabs.*

The highest land runs from Harare to the mountain massifs of **Nyanga**, **Bvumba** and **Chimanimani** flanking Mozambique. Everywhere there are the remains of Shona stone-walled villages, or *mazimbabwe*, and from earlier times, the exquisite rare paintings of the San hunter–gatherers.

Thirty-five percent of Zimbabwe is lowveld country, which fringes the country's borders and the prime wilderness areas of **Kariba** and **Gonarezhou**, and mostly lies below 915m (3000ft). A feature of the lowveld is the cream of tartar, or *umkhomo* in Ndebele, a massive tree with a circumference of up to 28m (90ft). Better known as the baobab, it looks as if God planted it upside down, roots sticking in the air.

Safari game conservancies (huge private game reserves), the country's best beer, 'Hunters', and cattle all come from the lowveld area stretching from the Shashe–Limpopo rivers and Thuli safari area in the southwest round to Gonarezhou and the Save River in the southeast. The heart of this area centres on **Chiredzi** and **Triangle** where sugar cane is grown. Two main roads from Bulawayo and Harare converge through the lowveld, heading for Beitbridge and South Africa.

Mountains and Rivers

The southeast and the northwest of Zimbabwe are laced with rivers, each hurrying to join the two big ones, the **Limpopo** and the **Zambezi**.

The Zambezi frames practically the entire northern edge of Zimbabwe for 715km (444 miles), and encompasses the upper rapids, **Victoria Falls**, **Lake Kariba** and

---

BAOBABS AND WILD HONEY

Baobabs can be up to 3000 years old. The tree's seed pod looks like a castanet, and the seeds are in a powdery pulp inside (young boys sell them by the roadside). Dead baobab trees have been known to sometimes burst into flame through spontaneous combustion. Some of the tastiest honey comes from bees who have collected nectar from the tree's waxy, white flowers. Small farmers, particularly in the Save valley, hollow out tree trunks to make log hives which are then hauled up into the cleft of a tree. The honey is collected at night by the farmer, who strips to the waist and removes large roundels of honey and wax.

- There are 76,000 elephant in Zimbabwe.
- An adult bull can weigh up to 6000kg (13,230 lb) and eats 300kg (662 lb) of grass and bark in one day.
- Best observation platforms are near Main Camp, Hwange, or on the Zambezi's flood plains.
- At Mana Pools, elephant browse around the chalets, shaking trees for pods, sometimes standing on their hind legs to reach the tasty winter-thorn acacia.
- Gonarezhou (place of elephants) boasts the largest beasts – but is notorious for poachers.
- Elephant are partial to the fruit of the wild almond, marula tree and ilala palm. They can ransack a camp if they smell oranges.
- In hunting parlance, the 'big five' are elephant, buffalo, rhino, lion and leopard.

Mana Pools. Dinosaurs used to walk its valley floor 150 million years ago. The river's upper section may once have flowed south into what is now the Makgadikgadi Pans of Botswana.

Rising in northwest Zambia, the Zambezi crosses into Angola, collecting rivers along its course, which further downstream include the Chobe in Botswana, the Sanyati in Lake Kariba, the Kafue and Luangwa in Zambia, and the Shire from Malawi and Mozambique. Mupata, on the Zambezi near Mana Pools, was at one time being considered as a site for another hydroelectric scheme, but has since been shelved in favour of the Batoka gorge (thus saving the wildlife in the Zambezi flood plain). The decision to go ahead with the new site will, unfortunately, end much of the white-water rafting.

In spite of the Zambezi and Limpopo's two great river systems, water often poses a problem in Zimbabwe. The rainy season is short, with brief heavy storms and rapid run-off, thus drought is always a possibility. Although some 7000 dams have been constructed, the second-largest city, Bulawayo, is still in great need of an adequate and reliable supply. There is some hope of using the Zambezi in the future.

Right: *Elephants gather around a waterhole in Hwange National Park. The area is also home to great numbers of buffalo, zebra, giraffe, antelope and around 25 different kinds of predator.*

Climate

Although technically in the tropics, Zimbabwe's altitude allows for a **temperate** climate that is much drier and cooler than the norm for Africa. During good years, there is enough wind, sufficient annual rain and seldom less than seven to nine hours of sunshine daily.

COMPARATIVE CLIMATE CHART	HARARE				ZAMBEZI RIVER				EASTERN HIGHLANDS			
	SUM JAN	AUT APR	WIN JULY	SPR OCT	SUM JAN	AUT APR	WIN JULY	SPR OCT	SUM JAN	AUT APR	WIN JULY	SPR OCT
MAX TEMP. °C	26	26	22	29	29	29	25	33	22	20	16	22
MIN TEMP. °C	16	13	7	15	18	14	6	17	13	10	5	11
MAX TEMP. °F	79	78	71	84	85	84	76	91	41	68	32	72
MIN TEMP. °F	61	55	44	58	65	57	42	63	55	51	42	52
HOURS SUN	7	8	9	9	7	9	10	9	6	8	8	9
RAINFALL in	8	1.5	0	1.5	5	1	0	3	10	2	1	2
RAINFALL mm	192	42	2	38	125	23	0	24	255	60	18	51

The weather is largely dictated by low- and high-pressure systems moving in a southeasterly direction past the South African coast. Being in the southern hemisphere, Zimbabwe has its winter, or cool months, from mid-May to mid-August, when the temperature drops to freezing at night and frost is regular.

Hail comes with **thunderstorms** in September through November, even on Lake Kariba. One year, a fisherman in a powerboat received two black eyes as a result of driving hail! Tobacco-growers have learnt that to ignore hail insurance is to take a gamble; insurance is almost as essential for farmers of winter wheat, cotton, maize and mountain fruit.

Spring is a **hot, dry** season from mid-August to October, followed by a **rainy summer**. Magnificent cloud formations accompany dramatic thunderstorms beginning in October. Autumn, during April and May, is a pleasant dry, transitional period that immediately follows the lush growth brought on by the rains.

Plant Life

Most distinctive are the country's vast tracts of indigenous trees (see p. 10) such as **msasa** and **munondo**, prevalent on the highveld, and the butterfly-leaved **mopane** in Matabeleland and the lowveld. The msasa, in particular, is exceptionally beautiful when it forms a filigreed silhouette against a blood-red sky, or in spring, when new leaves kaleidoscope from fawn to claret, often

---

HOT AND COLD YEARS

Having a temperate climate, Zimbabwe doesn't normally experience significant extremes, but naturally there are exceptions:
• Although frost is regular during the winter months, the last recorded major snowfall was in August 1935.
• October is known as 'suicide month' because of its oppressive heat, and no rain showers bring relief.
• The hottest temperature ever recorded in Zimbabwe was 46°C (115°F) at Kariba.
• The coldest was -11°C (12°F) in the Matobo National Park.
• October's violent thunderstorms regularly take their toll: more people have been killed by one bolt of lightning than in any other country (at the last count, the figure stood at 21).

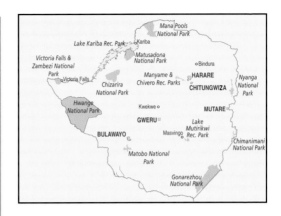

ZIMBABWE'S INDIGENOUS WOODLAND TREES

- **Msasa** (*Brachystegia spiciformis*); Shona name, musasa; common in Mashonaland; very striking in autumn.
- **Mopane** (*Colophospermum mopane);* Ndebele name, mopane; widespread in lowveld and Matabeleland; butterfly-shaped leaves.
- **Munondo** (*Julbernardia globiflora*); Shona name, munhondo; most widespread of Zimbabwe's trees.
- **Nyanga flattop** (*Acacia abyssinica*); tall umbrella tree growing in clumps, only in Eastern Highlands.
- **Paperback thorn** (*Acacia sieberana*); Shona name, Muunga; throughout Zimbabwe; creamy ball flowers.
- **Wild fig** (*Ficus burkei*); occurs on *kopjes*, ant hills and woodland areas.
- **Monkey orange** (*Strychnos spinosa*); grows in open woodland; ripe yellow fruit resembles grapefruit, but has hard shell; seeds poisonous.

Opposite: *One of the few remaining black rhino to have escaped the attentions of poachers in the Zambezi valley. This one was photographed in the Matusadona National Park, on the edge of Lake Kariba.*

providing a carpet of fire against a hillside or through a mountain valley. The highveld also has exotic species that have been introduced, such as pine, wattle and gum.

The country's indigenous forest areas include the great **teaks** and **mukwas** (bloodwoods) seen around Hwange, while the montane forests of the Eastern Highlands, with their heavy rainfall, feature **red mahoganies** near Chipinge, and also support a rich array of birdlife.

As the woodlands and forests are under continuous pressure of encroachment and the local population's immediate need for firewood, great efforts have been made to conserve these tracts. National tree-planting days, the building of rural dwellings from brick, the use of coal in tobacco-curing furnaces, and the extension of electricity to rural areas have all helped towards preserving this natural heritage – but it is an ongoing struggle.

Also characteristic of Zimbabwe's varied habitats are the tall grasslands between the trees and granite outcrops; the grasses are often used for fencing and hut thatching. The country has over 5000 species of flowering plants and ferns, 400 of them wildflowers (often tiny). Many are used for medicinal or other purposes, and have vernacular names. **Flame lilies** (the country's national flower), **save stars**, the blood lily (which has spectacular red puff-ball blooms), **aloes** and a variety of **orchids** and **cycads** are particularly attractive.

Conserving Zimbabwe's Wildlife Heritage

Thousands of years ago, far from Harare at Charewa, in a high *kopje* cave, a Stone Age San hunter–gatherer painted a picture of a rhino hunt. These rhino will have died to enable the little people to survive.

Today, however, man is not motivated by survival or the balance of nature, but by greed. In 1984, Zimbabwe had 3000 black rhino, the continent's largest herd. Ten years later poachers, particularly in the Zambezi valley, had reduced this number to 300. And this in spite of so many rhino already having been dehorned, as well as a ferocious defence action in which 200 poachers were killed. Unfortunately, rhino horn is an essential ingredient to traditional medicine in China and the Far East, a demand that refuses to be suppressed by Western scepticism or law-enforcement.

Attempts have been made to stop the slaughter of rhino by applying diplomatic pressure on the traditional medicine nations and by banning the horn trade. They have, over the last two decades, failed miserably. Some success has been achieved in translocating rhino to game ranches far from Zimbabwe's vulnerable borders for tourism purposes, others have been transported to overseas countries for captive breeding, and some to intensively protected wildlife areas. The real answer – if the Far East chemists' needs are to be met and the rhino to be saved – is controlled legal trade, which would pull the carpet out from under the profiteering middlemen. This applies to ivory too.

It is only fair to say that equally powerful arguments favour a total ban of horn and ivory trading, and it is here that the last battle is being waged.

The rhino has a right to survive in the wild, but time is running out; tough, clear-headed decisions need to be made soon, otherwise Zimbabwe and the rest of Africa will lose the last of these magnificent megaherbivores.

RHINO – IN BLACK AND WHITE

● There are two species of rhino: hook-lipped (black) and square-lipped (white). Despite their names, both have grey hides.
● The black rhino nibbles bushes and trees, the white grazes on the ground.
● The solitary black rhino weighs only a tonne, the white, which prefers to wander in small groups, two.
● Rhinos can create terrible fights over a female.
● A female black rhino has been known to kill a lion if it attacks her calf.
● Rhino horn is in fact compacted hair growing out of the animal's skin, not an extension of its skull.
● A gold-plated carved rhino was discovered 1000 years ago across the Limpopo at Mapungubwe, site of a large Iron Age town in South Africa.

ROCK ART

The San hunter–gatherers, known popularly as Bushmen, left a valuable record – paintings considered to be of great artistic merit – that reflected their lifestyle, the hunting of animals and the ritual trance-inducing dances in which they made contact with their god. Earth-toned paints were created by mixing crushed iron ore with clays and plant matter, sometimes animal fat or the yolk of an ostrich egg. Using very fine brushes, the paints have endured amazingly well. Zimbabwe boasts one of the most prolific collections of rock art in Africa.

HISTORY IN BRIEF

The first Zimbabweans were Stone Age nomadic hunter-gatherers who lived in the open bush, shared common tasks, had no harvest to worry about, and no desire to amass riches. We know them as **San** although the present !Kung of Botswana refer to themselves as Zhun!twasi, 'the real people'.

The San decorated their temporary dwellings, rock faces and caves with brilliant art depicting the hunt, their spirituality and their lifestyles. There may be 30,000 such sites in Zimbabwe.

At about the time of Christ and over a period of several centuries, some of these San may have exchanged their hunter–gatherer life in favour of a more settled existence, herding sheep and planting grain; others possibly developed pottery and iron-smelting skills.

Between 200BC and AD1000, **Bantu**-speaking agriculturalists and cattle herdsmen migrated south into Zimbabwe, absorbing and sometimes displacing the original San inhabitants. These people from the north also worked iron, made use of sophisticated pottery and lived in small villages and homesteads. The Bantu migrations down the African continent were sparked off, it seems, by the encroaching deserts of North Africa.

Below: *Ancient Bushman paintings on the Lowveld's vast Lone Star Ranch.*

People of the Setting Sun

About the time Alfred the Great was battling the Danes, Zimbabwe's central plateau was populated by the ancestors of the farmers and cattlemen we now call Shona. Based originally in game-rich plains on the edge of the Kalahari in the west, they came to be known as the 'people of the setting sun' from the Zulu expression *e shona langa* (where the sun sets). It is not clear whether they arrived as part of a Bantu migration or were in fact Stone Age San hunter–gatherers who had settled in the course of millennia into village life.

As the size of the cattle herds increased, the owners – together with those in charge of forging the valuable iron into hoes – grew in wealth and power. Gold mining also played its role in bringing riches to a few, as did trading with the coast. This surplus wealth and the emergence of powerful rulers had an important outcome: the construction of towering houses of stone, the likes of which had never been seen before in Africa.

Above: *Decorated earthenware jars displayed for sale in the remote Lundi area.*

Great Zimbabwe, Houses of Stone

Cattle barons built Great Zimbabwe, men who for centuries had perfected the art of guiding vast communal herds over the lush grazing lands of both the high- and lowveld, becoming extremely rich in the process.

They came from an area that was later to be called Matabeleland: Shona cattlemen and gold miners who had the ingenuity to draw on the country's varied skills – among them, copper working, iron smelting – and then to unify them, amass great wealth, and rule over the people.

By the 13th century they were building their exquisite houses of stone, *mazimbabwe*. Great Zimbabwe was built on the middleveld 27km (17 miles) southwest of today's Masvingo, at the crossroads of the seasonal grazing areas. At its height, the town harboured a population of up to 40,000 people and had a large army to guard its herds. Its influence stretched over much of modern Zimbabwe and a sizable portion of Mozambique.

> **ARTISTS IN CLAY**
>
> To make pots, the clay was dried, pulverized, then rinsed and mixed with water. The pliable earth was coiled upwards into various shapes, shaved down and ornamented before being dried in the sun, and finally fired in a pit of cow dung and bark. Geometric designs are often the same today as they were hundreds of years ago, but pottery pieces or shards reflecting minute changes are important to archaeologists in dating the people and their lifestyles.

Great Zimbabwe was occupied for 300 years. But by
1450 it had been abandoned; land and firewood exhaus-
tion, overpopulation, continuous drought and other economic criteria had taken over. It had perhaps become
impossible to motivate and coordinate the multiplicity of
peoples and skills needed to run a sophisticated state.

The **Mutapa** dynasty in the north and east was one of
the next great powers in Zimbabwe. Originally based at
Great Zimbabwe, the Mutapa had broken away during
its twilight years. Their *madzimambo*, or rulers, would in
the future be given the title Munhumutapa or 'master
pillager'. Legendary tales of the 'monomotapas' and
their supposed wealth and empire were brought back
from Africa by the Portuguese; genesis, perhaps, of
the King Solomon's Mines stories.

Because the Matabeleland middleveld was rich cattle
country, the successors to Great Zimbabwe (around the
time that St Peter's in Rome was under construction)
built many new *mazimbabwe*, two of which were **Danangombe** and **Naletale**. The finest was **Kame**, the capital of
the new state (referred to by historians as Torwa).

Men of the Sea

Five hundred years ago Portuguese navigator Vasco da
Gama sailed from Lisbon to find a sea route around
Africa to India. This he did, and during the course of his

Right: *The main complex at
Great Zimbabwe.* **Opposite:**
*Lobengula, last king of the
Ndebele people.*

travels, he named Natal, in South Africa. In 1502 he landed at Sofala on the Mozambique coast.

The Swahili traders persuaded the Portuguese that fabulous wealth akin to Ophir and King Solomon's Mines lay in the interior, ruled by Munhumutapa, and for the next 300 years many a Portuguese explorer, trader and missionary ventured forth in anticipation of these legendary riches.

Eventually they set up permanent trading posts. Maize from the Americas was introduced (today it is the nation's staple), as well as lemons from India, the rootstock of modern-day Mazowe oranges and fruit squash. Not many of the trading post dwellings have been excavated; the largest is the 16th-century trading-fair village in the old gold-producing area of Mazowe.

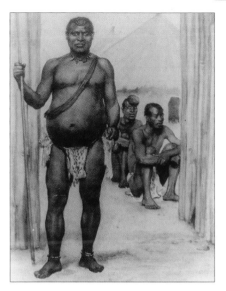

Man has, through the centuries, been partial to rape, pillage and plunder. At about the time the *Mayflower*, which had set sail from Plymouth with the Pilgrim Fathers on board, landed in America, the **Rozvi** destroyer–plunderers united under their 'changamire' (in those days meaning 'chief') and set off south in the 1680s to create mayhem among the **Torwa**. They occupied the houses of stone at Danangombe (or Dhlo Dhlo) and Naletale, leaving the Torwa culture more or less intact, to continue their fights with the Mutapa in the north and the Portuguese in the east.

Shaka's Rise to Power

In 1818 Shaka, an astute warrior and tactician based further south in what is now known as Zululand, formed the **Zulu** nation in a maelstrom of violence, scattering clans to all points of the compass.

Hightailing it north were the tribes of Soshangane, Zwangendaba and finally Mzilikazi's Khumalo – named

---

KING SOLOMON'S MINES

To Western man, historical Zimbabwe was the biblical land of Ophir, embracing hidden riches and gold. He was not altogether wrong, although initially very little gold was found. Of the more than 6000 deposits that have been worked since the English first came to Zimbabwe in 1890, most had been worked as early as the 11th century by the Shona before them. Modern mining is undertaken by large companies, but there are still individual prospectors, and along the rivers, outlaw panners who offer their furtive gleanings of gold dust in porcupine quills. Besides gold, emeralds, semiprecious stones and diamonds are exported.

Ndebele by their victims, meaning 'those who disappear behind long shields'. This wave of migration was to see the Ndebele settled in the west of Zimbabwe in 1837, now the second-largest language group, and the one that finally destroyed the last of Changamire–Rozvi hegemony on the high plateau.

Above: *Sentimentalized sketch of an incident in the Ndebele rebellion in 1896.*

CECIL JOHN RHODES

Cecil John travelled to South Africa because of poor lungs. He made a fortune in diamonds there, became prime minister of the Cape Colony, connived in the run-up to the Jameson Raid (which led to the Boer War) and set out to extend British influence from Cape Town to Cairo. One of his Zimbabwe homes is now a hotel in Nyanga's mountain park. Still today, part of the fortune he amassed contributes towards putting bright young students through Oxford University. His tomb sits atop another of his estates, World's View in the Matobo National Park, where his 'immense and brooding spirit' hovers with the black eagles over Zimbabwe's turbulent history.

The Coming of the Europeans

The first Westerner to enter Zimbabwe was the Portuguese explorer **Antonio Fernandes** in 1513. The first Englishman was a Scot, missionary **Robert Moffat**, in 1854, followed by his son-in-law **David Livingstone**.

Livingstone and writer **Henry Stanley**'s heroic tales of darkest Africa, **Frederick Courtney Selous**' ivory hunting, artist **Thomas Baines**' gold find, and **Adam Renders**' report on Great Zimbabwe launched a wholesale grab for the region's presumed wealth.

Within 40 years the British had occupied the country – and like so many before, imposed their culture and language. By 1895, Zimbabwe was known outside Africa as Rhodesia, after mining magnate Cecil John Rhodes; Salisbury was the capital.

Rhodesia versus Zimbabwe

Taxes, forced labour and appropriation of land were the sparks for a war of liberation, or *chimurenga*. After one defeat in 1893, the Shona and Ndebele (traditionally enemies) combined to drive out the Europeans. Led by Mhondoro spirit mediums Mbuya Nehanda and Sekuru Kaguvi, many of the settlers were killed, but against their superior and ruthless fire power, the *chimurenga* fizzled. For the duration of the next 85 years, Zimbabwe was ruled by and for the British.

The 19th-century competition among European powers for territory in Africa left a huge part of the world ruled by the 'great Queen across the waters'. In Rhodesia, which had seen a steady inflow of European immigrants, the early years were tough. 'Next year will be better' was the oft-expressed hope, but it seldom was.

The Rhodesians – laid-back, convinced of their superiority and their civilizing mission, sport-loving but none too fond of books – regarded themselves as frontier folk, the rugged outer fringes of the Empire. They believed they had a natural right to the best land, jobs, government and privilege. It was a recipe for disaster.

The year 1957 saw the emergence of the Southern Rhodesian African National Congress with Joshua Nkomo as president. By the end of 1960, 18 African countries had become independent of their European powers. In 1963 the nationalist movement split into the Zimbabwe African National Union (ZANU) and the Zimbabwe African People's Union (ZAPU); furious rivalry developed. Meanwhile the white Rhodesians pressed the British government to give them independence on their narrow terms.

Ian Smith, a farmer, became prime minister of Southern Rhodesia in 1964. He was determined to grab independence unilaterally if necessary, which he did on 11 November 1965. It was to be the cue for the demise of white political authority.

War of Resistance

The British government deliberated, the United Nations imposed mandatory sanctions, and the Shona and Ndebele took to the gun.

The first major battle was that of Chinhoyi, near the small

> **MBUYA NEHANDA**
>
> The 1896–97 revolt against the European settlers was led by Grandmother Nehanda. A spirit medium who was captured and hung, Nehanda prophesied that her bones would rise again, and her memory was inspirational in the second *chimurenga*, against the Rhodesians. In 1972, one of the four sectors of the Northeastern Front was code-named Nehanda ('Hurricane' to the Rhodesians); a new spirit medium – an old woman – was carried from her home to Chifombo Camp on the Mozambique–Zambia border to inspire the fighters. A handsome metal sculpture of Nehanda stands in the National Archives.

Below: *Ian Smith, Southern Rhodesia's prime minister.*

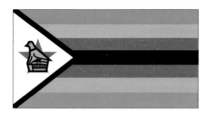

Opposite: *Zimbabwe's post-Independence leaders – formerly opponents, now colleagues: Robert Mugabe* **(right)**, *premier and president since 1980; and his vice-president Joshua Nkomo* **(left)**.

farming town, on 28 April 1966. But the Zimbabweans were ineffectual until the 1970s when rural infiltration on classic guerrilla lines was combined with the logistical support of a Mozambique free of Portuguese control. The South Africans pressured Ian Smith to negotiate, young men – *vakomana,* or 'lads' – slipped over the border in increasing numbers for training, while every Rhodesian had to spend more and more time patrolling the bush.

Gradually the war approached the cities. Every night on television, those killed were announced. Women fought alongside the men on both sides, whether as guerrilla commander in the field or homestead wife.

A million rural farmers were forced into protected villages to cut off food and supplies to the guerrillas. The Rhodesian military launched attacks into nearby Mozambique. On 9 August 1976 a thousand people died at Nyadzonia, a thousand more in Chimoio a year later. Rhodesian Intelligence also created the Renamo army in Mozambique, a move that was to lead to 15 years of civil war in that country.

In the mid-1970s, following the expulsion of the Portuguese regimes in Angola and Mozambique, the United States and South Africa pushed hard for a settlement, and Smith made overtures to the leaders of the two main liberation groups, Robert Mugabe of ZANU and Joshua Nkomo of ZAPU (the two in fact decided to join forces and formed the Patriotic Front). These moves came to nothing and instead, in 1978, Smith reached an accord with international Zimbabwean politician, Bishop Abel Muzorewa. The accord was rejected by the Patriotic Front, which continued to wage war.

Eventually, the pressure became too much. An all-party conference was called in London and signed on 21 December 1979. Free elections followed in February 1980, and Robert Mugabe became Zimbabwe's first prime minister. At midnight on 17 April, the British flag was run down for the last time.

Nearly 8000 people died in the last year of war, 27,000 in total; 150,000 had become refugees. It was a terrible price, but the chirpy young guerrilla *vakomana* could now come home, the weary Rhodesian could unlock his high farm gate, and hope could blossom once again in the high skies of the plateau country.

The Birth of Zimbabwe

On 18 April 1980, 90 years after Cecil John Rhodes' pioneer wagons rolled across Zimbabwe, the Shona and Ndebele had finally achieved independence; Zimbabwe had become Africa's 50th state. Jubilation erupted, and Prime Minister Robert Mugabe, in a masterful television performance, reassured all that there was place in Zimbabwe for both the winners and the losers.

The economy began to pick up, and although two-thirds of the Rhodesians had left, the commercial farmers – the economic backbone of the country – stayed. Conflicts between Mugabe and Nkomo's parties resulted in considerable bloodshed in Matabeleland, but these were eventually resolved in 1987 with the signing of a unity accord, Mugabe becoming executive state president and Nkomo one of two vice-presidents. Scandal and corruption in the late 1980s among the ruling élite resulted in court trials and disgrace. There is still corruption, but it is often well investigated in the national albeit state-dominated press.

Mugabe, who has always been a staunch advocate of the one-party state, had hoped for one in Zimbabwe, but opposition – including from within his own party – persuaded him otherwise. He had also begun to implement a centralized command economy, but this, too, was abandoned under pressure from Zimbabwean businessmen, the World Bank, and Western donor countries in favour of a market economy.

ROBERT MUGABE

Robert Gabriel Mugabe, son of a carpenter, born 21 February 1924 in Southern Rhodesia; trained as a teacher, gained first taste of nationalist politics at South Africa's University of Fort Hare; spent some years in Ghana, returned to Zimbabwe and helped form breakaway ZANU party (from Nkomo's ZAPU) in 1963; arrested for 'subversive speech' in 1964, spent 10 years in prison, acquired number of law degrees; during imprisonment succeeded in deposing ZANU's leader, Rev Sithole, in coup in 1974; freed in 1975, became joint leader with Joshua Nkomo of Patriotic Front; after negotiations in London ended 1975–1979 civil war, Mugabe won landslide election victory to become first prime minister of Zimbabwe.

HISTORICAL CALENDAR

3000BC–AD300 Caves and rock overhangs painted by hunter–gatherers.

200BC–AD300 Arrival of Bantu agriculturalists and herdsmen; by AD800, central plateau occupied by these ancestors of the Shona.

1200–1450 Rise, construction and abandonment of Great Zimbabwe.

1450–1650 Mwenemutapa (master of ravaged lands) dynasty in northeastern Zimbabwe and part of Mozambique.

1502 Vasco da Gama lands at Sofala and in 1513 Antonio Fernandes is first Westerner to enter Zimbabwe.

1480–1680 Torwa state rules in south and west, based at Kame.

1680s Changamire–Rozvi (destroyer–plunderers) conquer the Torwa.

1838 Mzilikazi and Ndebele conquer the southwest.

1854 Robert Moffat (first Briton to Zimbabwe) visits Mzilikazi.

1855 David Livingstone 'discovers' the Victoria Falls.

1868 Hunter Adam Render sees Great Zimbabwe ruins.

1890 Cecil John Rhodes' Pioneer Column invades Zimbabwe; country named Rhodesia.

1896 First chimurenga led by two spirit mediums; resistance is crushed, Matabele chief, Lobengula, is defeated.

1902 Cecil John Rhodes buried in Matobo Hills.

1923 Southern Rhodesian whites vote not to join Union of South Africa.

1957 Joshua Nkomo leads Southern Rhodesian African National Congress.

1965 Ian Smith's UDI results in international sanctions and guerrilla warfare.

1966 First battle of the second chimurenga, near Chinoyi.

1980 End of 14-year-war (in which 27,000 died) with Zimbabwean Independence; Robert Mugabe first prime minister.

1987 Unity Accord between main political rivals Mugabe and Nkomo.

1994 Relations between Zimbabwe and South Africa formally improve.

Currently uppermost in people's minds, the question of land ownership rights is an ongoing one. True, too few farmers whose forebears took whatever land they fancied are holding too much land. In rural areas there is crowding among small farmers. But the ruling party is only too aware that by strangling the golden goose, little of value is achieved. It is an issue that will, of economic necessity, be resolved slowly.

There being peace in Mozambique, independence in Namibia and a new dispensation in South Africa, Zimbabwe looks to clear skies, politically and economically.

GOVERNMENT AND ECONOMY

Zimbabwe's ruling party, the Zimbabwe African National Union (Patriotic Front) – ZANU (PF) – aimed to revolutionize the imbalance of land, health and education, and to jerk its people up by the bootstraps of a command economy, promising political paradise. But Robert Mugabe inherited a largely Western and British system – and an economically sophisticated country that was the envy of many in Africa. And he is a pragmatist. Cabinet and civil service use the old revolutionary term 'comrade', but the judiciary, banking system, style of government and parliament is a replica of Westminster. That Zimbabwe's bewigged Mister Speaker has to exhort snoozing ministers to do their homework is the stuff of wry novelists (Jeffrey Archer has effectively brought a smile to people's lips with his treatment of this subject in his novels).

A small but persistent opposition does exist, strengthened by the presence of a variety of hard-hitting opposition newspapers.

Some are prone to praise Zimbabwe by comparison with other African states, but the democratic process in Zimbabwe has flaws. The presidency is not limited to a fixed number of terms, undue reverence is thus accorded the leadership, and political change vital to democracy and the avoidance of disillusion will not come easily.

Robert Mugabe has a knack for reconciliation: he did it for the whites in 1980, he brought Nkomo – his main political opponent – into his government, played a major role in the Mozambique and Angola peace talks, and in 1993 adroitly diffused a flare-up of Ndebele discontent in Bulawayo. Mugabe has invited whites into his government and only occasionally sends a frisson of fear through their farming community when he talks about redistributing land. They are big enough to cope with it.

Economic Wealth

The new government moved fast to establish its control of the economy, thus creating only partially competent parastatals, state-purchased enterprises, red tape, price controls, and draconic currency exchange. The government reached the point where they controlled 60% of exports, 100% of imports and they employed 25% of the national workforce. Twelve years later, having stretched itself on defence, education and health, Zimbabwe began

---

MINING

Diamonds in the Beitbridge area are Zimbabwe's rising star, although gold still holds primary place. The country is the world's 12th-largest producer of gold, and its university has an Institute of Mining Research. Modern mining accounts for 40% of exports. Other minerals include asbestos, chrome, nickel, coal, copper, platinum, silver and many more. Added to this is a variety of precious stones, including the big four: diamonds, emeralds, rubies and sapphires. The wet-spring-grass hue of Zimbabwe's Sandawana emeralds is renowned. So far, the largest uncut diamond found in Zimbabwe is 37.5 carats.

Below, left: *Rough and polished gemstones.* **Below, right:** *An uncut diamond.*

to turn it around. Today one can obtain forex to any amount (at a price), the civil service is being reduced, food subsidies have been removed, and a much more liberalized ESAP plan for the economy is in action.

Those at the poorer end of the spectrum, perhaps inevitably, are taking the brunt in unemployment, rising food prices and inflation (24% in 1994). In spite of this, a burgeoning population, plus tough World Bank and European trading regulations, Zimbabwe has the basic infrastructure for economic success.

Manufacturing

After South Africa, Zimbabwe's range of products is the second largest in sub-Saharan Africa and covers practically everything: car assembly, trailers, rubber tyres, shoes, clothing, paper, liquor, pharmaceuticals, cement, steel, canned foods, construction equipment and fertilizers. All these are an indication of the extent of the country's industrial base.

Many more foreign goods are now coming into the country, giving the local industrialists stiff competition; after 30 years of sanctions and restrictions there is little now one cannot buy. Second-hand cars are still expensive and the price of imported wines, exorbitant. Scotch, however, is cheaper than in Scotland!

Energy and Water

Most of Zimbabwe's power comes from Lake Kariba. Hwange's thermal power stations at Hwange Colliery provide much of the rest. Zimbabwe's coal reserves stand at some 30,000 million tonnes – enough to last

EASY TRAVELLING

Zimbabwe's communication structure covers an excellent network of well-maintained roads and 3400km (2113 miles) of railway track between all the towns. After the government, the National Railways of Zimbabwe is the single largest employer in the country. A good road network is important to Zimbabweans, whose culture of working in the city, yet maintaining a small farm in the country, revolves around the rural bus. These buses are a common sight on Zimbabwe's roads, whether tar or gravel. Packed, colourful and resplendent with rooftop luggage, they cover every corner of the country.

Air Zimbabwe, with its fleet of mainly Boeing 737 aircraft, operates a sophisticated schedule of services to Victoria Falls, Hwange, Kariba, Johannesburg and Bulawayo, as well as flights to Europe and Australia.

another 10,000 years. Households only use about 15% of the electricity generated, the bulk being utilized by construction, manufacturing and transport. The rural areas are still short of electricity, presenting an ongoing threat to the country's tree cover; but in general most urban households operate on electricity.

An ethanol plant – the first in Africa – at Triangle in the lowveld produces 40 million litres (8.8 million gall) per annum from sugar cane, which is blended with petrol. The word 'blend' is on every gas-station pump in the country. Water is provided by Zimbabwe's 21 major dams and 7000 others.

Social Sciences

Apart from education, the major area of government expenditure is health. Public Health services are free for lower-income groups; traditional medicine is recognized and encouraged. Zimbabwe has lost a lot of its Harare-trained doctors to higher salaries in neighbouring countries, thus the rural areas are largely staffed by ex-patriates. Medical facilities and hospitals are generally good: there are some 300 hospitals and 500 clinics throughout the country. Private medicine is particularly good. Childhood diseases, malaria and AIDS are a problem. Social Welfare is controlled by the government and there are some 900 regis-tered welfare organiza-tions in the country.

In the towns there is a shortage of low-cost housing, while in the rural areas, many Zimbabweans live in traditional *musha* of circular thatched huts. Clean borehole water and electricity at growth points are priority issues that have been placed high on the agenda.

> ### AN APPLE A DAY
>
> Zimbabwe is competing aggressively on world fruit and vegetable markets, with much of its produce packed and marked for Safeways or Marks and Spencer in the UK. The country imports neither commodity. Provided one is happy to move with the seasons, farm-grown fruits and vegetables number over 70. Among the more exotic fruits are mangoes, sugar cane, bananas, kiwi fruit, avocados, pineapples, litchis and granadillas. Flowers are also now a major export industry.

Opposite: *Zimbabwe boasts a highly developed rail network, operated for the most part by diesel traction.*
Below: *Harvesting tea in the fertile Honde valley.*

THE PEOPLE

It is often remarked upon by visitors to Zimbabwe that the people of the country display a particularly happy nature; they are quick to laugh and are relaxed with foreigners, talking willingly and easily with them.

Most Zimbabweans are **Shona**, a substantial minority **Ndebele**. English is one of the official languages, and is spoken by everyone, although a total of seven languages is spoken in the country. Of the population of 11 million, 25% live in urban areas. Harare, with its satellite Chitungwiza, accounts for more than 50% of the population. Some 60,000 Zimbabweans have English as their native language and Europe as their roots. They live mainly in Harare (32,000) and Bulawayo (16,000).

Many of the elderly live in the rural areas, while 20% of the rural population live on large commercial farms. There are small groups of **Asian** origin and **Afro-European** descent. Urban drift, the cities being perceived as the place to obtain work, is a major sociological problem and a constant threat to old-fashioned values in the face of fast food, fast living and crowded conditions.

SELF-HELP SUCCESS

Drought and economic depression have forced many Zimbabweans to develop new skills. This is particularly so in the communal areas where the soils are poor, the rains unreliable, the land overpopulated, and agriculture no longer able to fulfil the people's needs – especially those of women whose husbands may have abandoned them while working in town. The **Weya Community Training Centre** 170km (106 miles) from Harare was started to supplement incomes from subsistence farming. Dressmaking was not enough, and they now produce superb paintings, sold all over the world, tel: (14) 703251/228.

Language

Chilapalapa is a politically incorrect patois; Ndebele based, it is used mainly on commercial farms between employer and worker. An Afro-European slang laced with laconic humour makes use of such phrases as 'grazed by a flatdog' to describe being attacked by a crocodile, and 'Eh, petrol China, chuck some sky in my rounds', which is essentially asking the petrol attendant to put air in one's tyres.

Shona, with its six main dialects, is the mother tongue to 67% of the population, while **Ndebele** is spoken by 15%. Town Shona or chiHarare is a freewheeling mix of dialects and some English. Quite a few Shona speakers use public-school **English**; it can be a disadvantage politically, a bonus in business. All the street signs and nearly every newspaper is in English; it is the language of television news, policemen and taxi drivers. City slickers like to josh back and forth in all the main languages, especially if there's an audience.

City Lifestyles

Clothes are important to the city dweller. The population being young, to look sharp is cool. Hairstyles run the full gamut of Africa, the Caribbean and Harlem.

To own a car is a devout goal not often achieved. Zimbabwe's cities are an action museum of ancient makes. It is also four-wheel-drive territory. A proliferating diplomatic and donor community prefer land cruisers for goodly works in the rural areas.

Zimbabweans are not good drivers and have a penchant for traffic-light jumping. Watch out for emergency taxis and minibuses who make their own law and the urban elite who consider themselves above it. Drinking and driving is also a serious problem.

Burial societies and women's church groups do much to provide

---

FODDER FOR THE MIND

- Of Zimbabwe's total population of 11 million, 50% are under 15.
- At Independence, 820,000 children were in primary school; today there are over two million.
- At the same time, 66,000 children were in secondary school; today there are 700,000.
- The **University of Zimbabwe** in Harare offers science, medicine, engineering, veterinary science, and many other faculties. Near Mutare is the **Africa University**, and in Bulawayo the **National University of Science and Technology**. Two more universities are under consideration.
- Zimbabwe has five agricultural colleges and four technical colleges.
- 14% of Zimbabwe's budget is spent on education.

Opposite, left: *A Shona man in colourful garb.*
Opposite, right: *Ndebele tribal dancing.*

SPEAK THE LANGUAGE		
English	**Shona**	**Ndebele**
How are you?	makadii?	linjani?
Thank you	mazvita	siyabonga
How much?	i marii?	yimalini?
Yes/no	ehe/aiwa	yebo/hayi
Where?	kupi?	ngaphi?
One	potsi	okukodwa
Two	piri	okubili
Tea	tii	itiye
Bread	chingwa	sinkhwa
Beer	hwahwa	utshwala
Elephant	nzou	ndhlovu
Lion	shumbai/mhondoro	silwane

ZESTY ENTREPRENEURS

Women selling grilled maize, soapstone carvings on display in First Street, dog-basket makers at shopping centres, cobblers who will mend a suitcase for a song: whenever there is a concentration of passing people, there are small entrepreneurs. A Chaucerian cast of characters may include a bicycle mender at the side of a busy road, a tailor on the veranda of a country store, youngsters who repack fruit outside the supermarket, instant garages, plumbers, food vendors, sign- and coffin-makers or tree-cutters. There are bus-hawkers, emergency taxis and kerb-side hairdressers. This grass-roots capitalism is a vital ingredient in Zimbabwe's economy.

a form of security for marginalized families in the high-density suburbs that have mushroomed around the major cities. It is a story of rich and poor, rather than poverty, that grinds and betrays. In these suburbs, business innovation and pavement enterprises flourish.

Basic minimum wages have been introduced and the extended urban–rural family network still cushions the worst of economic hardship. The élite, of course, lead a sugared life in the leafy suburbs with electric gates, swimming pools and gleaming automobiles. But reaction to this is aspiration rather than envy.

With urbanization crime has increased, but it is seldom violent or armed, and police are much more evident on city streets; luxury cars destined for Zambia are the favourite target for the city's criminals.

Religion

Man has always believed there is a caring being guiding his life. Of the two largest religions in Zimbabwe, 50% consult traditional *midzimu* ancestors via Zvikiro, while 50% pray, as **Christians**, to Baba Jesus or *Mwari* (the 17th-century Rozvi term for God). Sometimes they revere both, as the humility and hospitality of a largely

rural people sits well with the best of Christian beliefs.

The first Christian missionary in Zimbabwe was the Jesuit Gonçalo da Silveira (his name was given to a large educational centre in Harare whose former members include today's president Robert Mugabe) in 1560, although many a Muslim trader had been to Zimbabwe earlier.

The Moffat family arrived in 1859 at Inyathi near Bulawayo. **Vapostori** and **Zion** church members are often seen praying beneath the trees in their white robes, holding shepherds' crooks.

There are also small **Jewish**, **Muslim** and **Hindu** communities, mainly urban based.

Sport and Recreation

Football means everything in Zimbabwe. To beat South Africa is delirium, to get booted out of the Africa Cup, devastating. Crowds of 45,000 are drawn to big games and

there are many professional teams. The only game children play in township streets or on dusty rural patches is soccer, using a ball of plastic remnants tied together with string. The Super League and four major club competitions are all sponsored by beer or cigarette companies; the Dynamos have often been the top team.

Horse racing is also an obsession in Zimbabwe, not because of the love for horses, but for the love of betting. The annual tote turnover is in excess of Z$40 million. May to July is the main season, **Ascot** in Bulawayo and **Borrowdale Park** in Harare the two venues.

In international competition, Zimbabweans have been successful in cricket, hockey, tennis and swimming. Golf has made Nicky Price and Mark McNulty famous; the country has 70 golf courses.

White-water rafting and cruising on the Zambezi is the most popular sport with visitors, while rugby, running and cycling are all available.

A Bookish Society

The drive to provide schooling for everyone has cost the country dearly, as jobs are not commensurate. But it is a long-term policy that should pay future dividends. In the interim it has spurned a wealth of writing: novels, short stories, poetry and a highly sophisticated media. There are two daily papers on sale in Harare and half a dozen weekly and monthly magazines. The *Financial Gazette*

Above: *Thoroughbreds pound the turf at Borrowdale racecourse.* **Opposite:** *The evangelical Pentecostal religious movement has thousands of adherents.*

DRUMBEAT

Drums, mbiras, rattles and marimbas have long been used in traditional spiritual ceremonies; the Christian church has adopted these too. The rhythm of shared chanting and individual harmony is always used in times of harvest, war, suffering, weddings and burials. Depending on the area and people, drums can be tall, in a flat tambourine-style or designed to stand on three legs. Belingwe drums are held between the legs. The Tonga drums, like all the Tonga people's lovely artefacts, are extremely decorative. The Shangaan drum is cylindrical and hung from the neck, and was beaten en route to war.

is a prominent weekly paper, and of the monthly magazines, *Horizon* is considered to be the best.

Mambo Press and Baobab Books are consistent publishers of local works. English-speaking writers who lived and worked in Zimbabwe include **Doris Lessing**, **Wilbur Smith** and **John Gordon-Davis**.

The first Shona novel published was by **Solomon Mutswairo Feso**; then came **Herbert Chitepo**'s epic poem 'Soko Risina Musoro' (street signs are graced with Chitepo's name). Both works were banned by Ian Smith's government. These writers were followed by **Patrick Chakaipa** (now Roman Catholic Archbishop of Harare), **Isaac Mopfu** and **Amos Mzilethi**.

Food and Drink

Zimbabwe's national dish is *sadza*, a stiff porridge made of white maize that's delicious when first cooked. It is usually eaten with a vegetable relish or meat. Meat is high on a Zimbabwean's food list, but there are few national dishes. A Coke and a bun is the worker's lunch while *chibage*, or cold mealie on the cob, is the road

Right: *Fresh fruit on sale in Harare's downtown market.* **Opposite:** *Lake Kariba is popular for its tranquil houseboat holidays.*

snack. There is a lot of 'nouvelle' stodge in the city with the ubiquitous chips, if not fish, as a basic staple. Fast-food outlets – Wimpy, Chicken Inn, Nando's Chicken-land – have infiltrated the cities, with home-grown varieties in the high-density suburbs.

Squash, pumpkin, rape (a sort of spinach) and cabbage are the main vegetables. Fruits are excellent and varied. Game meats are not universally eaten but can be found in restaurants. Fish from South Africa or Mozambique is largely a rich man's luxury; Kariba bream is available, although variable. Food is inexpensive both in markets, shops and restaurants. There are some 60 restaurants in Harare, half this number in Bulawayo, and hotel restaurants in all but the most remote of wildlife areas.

Although Zimbabwe has been producing wine for only 30 years, the country makes a wide range of wines for local consumption. Recently South African, Australian and European labels have been imported, and compete with local ones. Zimbabwean wines are inexpensive by Western standards. The whites can be good (the Meadows Estate label is considered to be the best), but the reds still have a way to go.

THE GOOD LIFE

Zimbabwe is hot country, which means lager country: the best beer is Hunter's from the lowveld, served cold (but difficult to obtain). The line-up of lesser froths includes Lion (Shumba), Carling, Pilsener, and the two locals, Zambezi and Bohlinger. Then there's the favourite, Castle, named after Cape Town's fort, and Chibuku, a traditional thick, opaque beer. Bottled beer is seen to represent sophistication, the good life. Both young white and Chitungwiza businessmen drink it mercilessly. Bottle openers are redundant in Zimbabwe: the cap is flipped off with the top of one's next bottle, a core cultural action that serves to define manhood. Beer often accompanies meat burnt over an open fire or braai.

2
Harare and Surrounds

Boulevards of flowing trees, the colourful attire of First Street shoppers and bright overhead sunlight are the hallmarks of Zimbabwe's capital city, **Harare**. A hundred years old and named after Chief Harava, Harare's concentration of high-rise buildings accessed by a sensible street grid lie on a lofty plateau, guaranteeing cool nights after sometimes stifling hot days.

Also a tapestry of sights and sounds is the city's afro-chic suburb of **Mbare**. Music both traditional and popular is a constant backdrop to life here. Ancient blasters play in small shops, buses attract customers by decibel level and young men promenade their girls, radio balanced in one hand.

Harare is generally the hub for safaris to Victoria Falls, Great Zimbabwe, Hwange National Park and the Zambezi Valley wilderness, but its **Queen Victoria Museum**, **National Archives**, and **Heroes' Acre** do give it the trappings of a modest metropolis. Local and world-acclaimed stone sculptors exhibit in Harare's **National Gallery** and **Chapungu** sculpture park.

Zimbabwe means 'houses of stone', and one's attention is immediately drawn to the stone *kopjes*, and to the balancing boulders (at Epworth, outside Harare) and stone ruins that are so characteristic of the country.

For wildlife enthusiasts, a clutch of private reserves offering big game are situated just an hour from the city. The **Mukuvisi Woodlands**, **Larvon Bird Gardens** and **Lake Chivero** also have their share of interesting bird- and wildlife to attract the nature-loving visitor.

CLIMATE

Harare is **sunny** most days of the year, although there can be prolonged overcast spells during the **rainy season** (November to March) accompanied by spectacular lightning and thunder displays. At 1470m (4823ft), Harare's high, dry plateau is always cool at night, cold during the winter months (June to August). As the country waits for the October rains, it can be uncomfortably hot. Harare probably has one of the world's most **equable** climates and certainly not what visitors expect in Africa.

Opposite: *Elegant night-scape of Zimbabwe's capital city, Harare.*

DON'T MISS

★★★ Mbare Musika Market
★★★ Excursion to the Tobacco
Sales Floors
★★★ Mukuvisi Woodlands:
elephant, 300 bird species
★★ Chapungu sculpture park
for stone sculptures
★★ Heroes' Acre: monument
to the Independence struggle
★★ Larvon Bird Gardens: 250
species, weekend teas
★ Picnic trip to Ewanrigg
Botanical Gardens: glorious
aloes and cycads
★ Drive to Ngomakurira
rock paintings
★ Game-viewing at Lake
Chivero Recreational Park;
take a packed lunch.

HARARE
Mbare, Africa City ★★★

Mbare is a poor-rich tin and mango suburb, and the country's largest bus terminus. Harare's smoothest pick-pockets and sidewalk entrepreneurs work this area; it is also a huge market of extravagant variety and colour.

During the 19th century, Chief Mbare, who had held sway on Harare Kopje, quarrelled with newcomer Chief Gutsa and was beheaded, apparently in single combat. His defeat, however, didn't prevent his name from being given to this throbbing, people-inundated suburb no visitor should miss. It lies just south of the city near Rufaro stadium and the Pioneer cemetery; hire a street kid to watch your car, and if your buying is heavy, you can even hire a wheelbarrow man.

Take in the ferociously competitive bus action – 50 garish monsters jostling for space and clientele. Beds, bicycles, chickens, cabbages are strapped on the roof and as many people crammed inside as the shrill-whistle conductor can get away with. All around, banana and single-cigarette hawkers shout, quarrel and laugh in Mbare hip street-slang. Above all this, wild Afro-music blares from the interior of half a dozen shops.

Best buys outside the main market are canvas com-rade bags, the carryall of rural Zimbabwe. Then to the

AFRICA BEAT

In Zimbabwe, popular African music goes back to the 1930s, and it's big business: *pungwes* (named after the clandestine wartime politic-ization sessions, now used for any all-night session of singing and dancing) can go on all night. Thomas Mapfumo, Oliver Mtukudzi, and the Bhundu Boys have all cut discs and have been well received in Europe. Skyline Motel and the three Highfield suburb venues, Club Sara-toga, Machipisa Nightclub and Mushandira Pamwe Hotel, are recommended. Traditional music is equally popular; mbira thumb piano, marimba and drums are the main instruments.

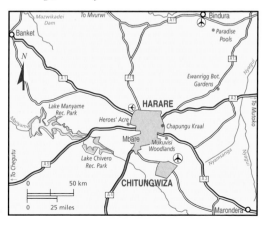

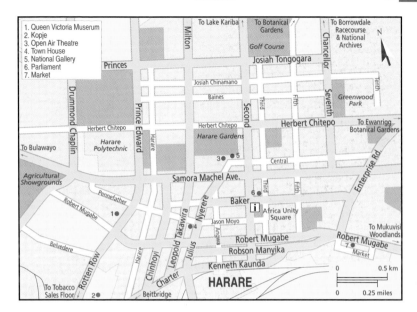

1. Queen Victoria Museum
2. Kopje
3. Open Air Theatre
4. Town House
5. National Gallery
6. Parliament
7. Market

Musika itself, acres of crafts, fresh vegetables, tobacco, second-hand clothes, mysterious *N'anga* herbal potions and some of the most colourful characters south of the kasbah. Revel in the frenetic activity; don't be scared but do be sensible about your purse. Around the corner is the **Canon Paterson Art Centre** (for stone carvings).

Tobacco Auctions ★★★

Tobacco-growing provides a livelihood for thousands of Zimbabweans and the country is one of the world's largest producers. It is cured in the high brick barns visible throughout the farming areas. Tobacco was grown in Zimbabwe in the 19th century and may have been introduced by the Portuguese. The tobacco floors, where long lines of baled tobacco are sold by quick-fire, walking-up-the-lines auction, make an interesting morning's outing.

The bales are opened so that buyers can feel, see and smell the tobacco. A starter sums up the bale's value and calls a figure to the auctioneer, who then starts a sing-song chant, pushing up the bids which are made by mysterious hand and facial movements by the buyers.

The **Tobacco Sales Floor** in Gleneagles Road, Willowvale (the largest in the world), holds auctions daily, from April to the end of October. Guided tours are available in the huge complex and visitors can observe the auctions. On an average morning 16,000 bales will be sold and up to 150 million kg (330.7 million lb) in a season.

Above: *Local stone sculpture is world renowned.*
Opposite: *The entrance to Chapungu sculpture park.*

Heroes' Acre **

A long and bloody war was fought in Zimbabwe to wrest control of the country from the European settlers who conquered it 100 years ago. The conflict, fought mainly by guerrilla warfare in the rural areas, lasted from 1976 to 1980 and resulted in over 25,000 deaths. A ceremonial burial ground, Heroes' Acre is the nation's monument to this terrible struggle. To Western eyes it does not have the appeal of a Nelson's Column, Voortrekker Monument or Arc de Triomphe, but those who fought in Vietnam will relate to its stark, black Mutoko granite. Sited on 57ha (140 acres) of woodland a few kilometres west of Harare, its main features are a bronze statue of the **Unknown Soldier** (comprising two men and a woman) looking out from a series of levels which lead up to the eternal flame at a height of 40m (130ft). There is a museum and bas relief murals depicting the conflict. Those buried near the huge amphitheatre include General Josiah Tongogara, commander of the largest army in the struggle.

Believed to be in South Africa is another statue of the Zimbabwean war: a Rhodesian 'troopie', made from spent cartridges. Perhaps one day in a final spirit of reconciliation it, too, will come home.

A permit to visit the site must be obtained; this is issued, while you wait, at the Ministry of Information, Public Relations Office, in Harare (located in Linquenda House, Baker Street). Brochures are also available.

Mukuvisi Woodlands ***

The Mukuvisi used to be Harare's 'skinny-dipping' hangout 60 years ago, before the river was forced underground by urban sprawl and seasonal factors; it's now the boundary of a 270ha (670 acres) game park off Glenara Avenue South, of which David Shepherd, the renowned elephant and African landscape artist, is a patron. The park has baby elephant, zebra, sable, wildebeest, eland, crocodile and waterfowl in a wildlife habitat of 160 tree species and 300 species of bird.

Almost the entire wildlife and conservation establishment of Zimbabwe joined hands to save the woodlands, and the headquarters of both the **Zimbabwe Wildlife Society** and the **Zambezi Society** are based here. There is a shop, Interpretive Centre, aviary display centre, game-viewing platform and guided trails through the bush.

Larvon Bird Gardens **

For the serious bird-watcher, aviaries are not normally a first choice, but for anyone keen to learn about the birds of Africa, Larvon Bird Gardens on the Bulawayo road is an ideal training ground before heading for the wilds. There are over 250 species in various walk-through aviaries, with a lake for waterfowl.

The larger birds such as vultures have ample room in which to stretch their prodigious wings; the lappet-faced vulture has the largest wingspan (2.7m; 8.8ft) and will dominate at kills, flapping, hopping and pecking off other vultures until it has had its fill.

CHAPUNGU

This reconstructed 19th-century Shona village on the eastern edge of Harare features African folk dancing at weekends, but its strength lies in its open-air sculpture park overlooking a lake. Here, internationally known Zimbabwean sculpture artists work on the lawns in verdite, granite, jasper and other stone. Chapungu is the Shona word for a bateleur eagle, considered to be the spirit messenger of the high savanna.

The nectar-feeding birds with their inquisitive curved
bills are some of the prettiest. They are fed on honey, vit-
amins and cereal. To feed the hoopoes, the staff have to
hunt for termites in nearby anthills! Teas are served
beside the lake at weekends.

Lake Chivero Recreational Park ★
Fish Eagle, Kingfisher and Mocking Chat are the names
of three of the National Parks' thatched lodges at Lake
Chivero Recreational Park, formerly Lake MacIlwaine,
37km (23 miles) from Harare. This is Harare's weekend
playground. The lake offers sailing and boating, and on
the southern shore is a game reserve with rhino, giraffe,
zebra and a variety of buck in the msasa-clad hills. There
are pony trails, fishing in the lake, and at Bushman
Point, rock paintings and well-marked walking trails.

Right: *A Burchell's zebra
at Lake Chivero, near
Harare.* **Opposite:** *The
blooms of the coral tree, a
familiar city sight.*

It is an ideal spot if one is spending a few days in Harare and has a car. The northern shore of the lake has sailing and boating clubs, and the attractive **Hunyani Hills Hotel**, as well as the nearby National Parks caravan and camp sites. If you prefer a peaceful environment, avoid weekends, which can be noisy.

Aloes for Africa at Ewanrigg *

Flaming aloes in the June–July winter months make a spectacular display in the Ewanrigg Botanical Gardens 41km (25 miles) from Harare off the Shamva road.

Led by the brash red-hot poker, aloes are part of the lilies of the field growing in a riot of 57 species in Ewanrigg. Walk from terrace to rockery, each with banks of flowers or shrubs, while the open paths, flanked by rolling lawns, lead to a herb garden, water garden, display of hybrid aloes and finally a profusion of bougainvillea, barberton daisies, fuchsias and bamboos. For the avid bird-watcher, there are also many long-beaked, nectar-sipping sunbirds.

An abundance of picnic and barbecue spots have been established, and it is possible to buy firewood. Plants can be purchased too. The Ewanrigg gardens are controlled by Zimbabwe's National Parks.

Ten minutes away lies Mermaid's Pool, known for its rock water-slide (although swimming is not recommended as it is bilharzia-infested).

DRUMMING SPIRITS

Ngomakurira on the Domboshawa Road (42km; 26 miles), meaning 'where the spirits beat the drums', is one of Zimbabwe's 6000 known rock-art sites. The paintings, done in shades of ochre on a sheer mountain cliff (follow the arrows to a choice of two sites) are of huge elephant and stick-like humans. Hunter–gatherer, or San, artists lived in Zimbabwe from 2000 to 20,000 years ago. A few of the !Kung people still live in the Kalahari desert.

Harare and Surrounds at a Glance

Normally sunny by day throughout the year, and because of the altitude, cool at night. **April** and **May**, and the winter months of **June** and **July**, are ideal; October's heat can be uncomfortable. Summer rains and thunderstorms are fairly consistent November through February.

Direct flights from London, Johannesburg, Australia and a variety of European and African capitals to **Harare airport**, 18km (11 miles) outside the city; contact Air Zimbabwe reservations, tel: (14) 575021, after hours, tel: (14) 737011. Air Zimbabwe operates excellent all-inclusive Flame Lily holiday packages to every destination in the country. Harare is also accessible from Johannesburg (South Africa) and neighbouring countries via an excellent **road** and **rail network**. A Silverbird **luxury bus** travels from Johannesburg to Harare twice weekly, tel: (14) 794777, or call Johannesburg, tel: (011) 3377215. A Mini-Zim Travel coach also runs three times a week, tel: (14) 7204261 or 46163, or call Johannesburg, tel: (011) 8330380.

Hourly **shuttle bus** links airport with Air Zimbabwe terminal in Harare. **Car-hire** firms represented; try Europcar, tel: (14) 752559;

Avis, tel: (14) 751542; Hertz, tel: (14) 704915, among others. Public bus transport is limited. **Taxis** outside hotels (try Rixi Taxi, tel: (14) 753080). **Air charter** for access to safari areas, Executive Air, tel: (14) 302184, fax: 32949. Express Motorways **buses** ply between the major cities, as do trains. You can also try an **emergency taxi** (ET) or minibus, or **hire a bicycle** from Bushtrackers, tel: (14) 733573.

Please note: Chancellor Avenue, site of the president's home, is blocked to all traffic between 18:00 and 06:00.

Generally speaking, a five-star city-hotel rating in Zimbabwe is lower than in Western cities. In some hotels, visitors are required to pay in non-Zimbabwean currency and at a higher rate than locals.

Monomatapa: attractive semicircular high-rise overlooking Harare gardens, restful pastel interiors, selection of good restaurants, contact the Zimbabwe Sun group, tel: (14) 704501, fax: 791920.
Meikles: elegant colonial; the original hunter, farmer and prospector's hotel, now considered among the best in Africa; Meikles' black London cabs available to visitors; tel: (14) 795655, fax: 707754.
Sheraton: massive entrance foyer is a soaring kaleidoscope of glass, gold, circular stair-

ways and chandeliers (known to taxi drivers as 'golden delicious'!); favourite of conference groups, movie makers and airline crews, tel: (14) 729771, fax: 728450.
Cresta Jameson: in the heart of Harare, has a good restaurant called Tiffanys, call the Cresta group, tel: (14) 703131, fax: 794655.
Harare Holiday Inn: small, friendly, easy parking; beaming bemedalled porters, tel: (14) 795611, fax: 735695.
Hunyani Hills: attractive hotel on the north shore of Lake Chivero, tel: (162) 2236.

Ranch and Farm Accommodation
Farm Holiday Association: country living, often with wildlife, tel: (14) 727879 or 791881, fax: 750754.

National Parks lodges: Fish Eagle, Kingfisher, Mocking Chat and others, contact National Parks central booking office, PO Box 8365, Causeway, Harare; tel: (14) 706077.
Bronte Garden Hotel: ideal for families, tel: (14) 796631, fax: 721429.
Sable Lodge: for backpackers, tel: (14) 726017.

There are over 60 restaurants in Harare; steaks are excellent, as is the range of fruit and local cheeses (try the Vumba brand produced in the Bvumba area). The national

Harare and Surrounds at a Glance

dish is the working man's *sadza* (stiff maize porridge) accompanied by relish.

Ramambo Lodge, BP House, Samora Machel Ave: African game meats, safari atmosphere, tel: (14) 792029.
Mandarin, Ivory House, Robert Mugabe Rd: simple but good Cantonese cuisine, tel: (14) 726227.
Aphrodite Taverna, Strathaven Shopping Cntr: Greek food, great decor, tel: (14) 335500.
Alexander's, Livingstone Ave, off Second St: cosy colonial dining room, tel: (14) 700340.
Guido's, Montague Shopping Cntr: Italian, inexpensive favourite, tel: (14) 723349.
Sitar, Newlands Shopping Cntr: run by an Indian family, tel: (14) 729132.

TOURS AND EXCURSIONS

City tours and surrounds: United Touring Company (UTC), tel: (14) 793701; Kalambeza Safaris, tel: (14) 723156.
Game and gold-panning safaris in Hippo Pools Umfurudzi safari area: tel: (14) 46861.
Golfing tours (seven-day): UTC, tel: (14) 793701.
Tobacco Auction Floor tours: Kalambeza Safaris, tel: (14) 723156.
Walking safaris in Mukuvisi Woodlands: tel: (14) 731596.
White-water rafting and canoeing on the Zambezi: run by several operators, but

Shearwater Adventures specializes in these tours, tel: (14) 735712, fax: 735716.

Wildlife Safaris
Of the many **safari operators**, two of the best are John Stevens, tel: (14) 48548, fax: 46113, and Flip Nicholson, tel/fax: (14) 738143.
Camping equipment (tents) can be hired from Rooneys, tel: (14) 703515; **fishing, hunting** and **outback gear** can be obtained from Master Angler, fax: (14) 750525, and Feredays, tel: (14) 751687, fax: 728316.
You can get **good maps** from the Surveyor General, tel: (14) 794545, and Book Centre shops; **permits** obtainable from National Parks, tel: (14) 707624.
(Make sure you take anti-malaria tablets; bring binoculars, suntan lotion, sunglasses, hat and walking shoes.)

USEFUL TELEPHONE NUMBERS

Automobile Association, Fanum House, Samora Machel Ave, tel: (14) 752779.
Chapungu open-air sculpture park, tel: (14) 47472.
Ewanrigg Botanical Gardens, tel: (174) 23720.

Harare Publicity Bureau, Africa Unity Square, tel: (14) 705085.
Lake Chivero Recreational Park, tel: (14) 706077.
Larvon Bird Gardens, outside Harare on Bulawayo road, tel: (14) 724745.
Live music: Skyline Hotel, tel: (14) 67588; Club Saratoga, tel: (14) 66620; Machipisa Nightclub, tel: (14) 62406; Mushandira Pamwe Hotel, tel: (14) 64356.
National Parks central booking office, tel: (14) 706077.
Public Relations Office, Ministry of Information, Linquenda House, Baker Ave, Harare, tel: (14) 706891.
Wildlife Society of Zimbabwe, Glenara Ave South, Mukuvisi Woodlands, tel: (14) 700451.
Zambezi Society, Mukuvisi Woodlands, tel: (14) 731596.
Zimbabwe Association of Tour and Safari Operators and **Zimbabwe Professional Hunters and Guides Association**, tel: (14) 733211, fax : 723230.
Zimbabwe Tourist Development Corporation, Tourism House, Cnr Fourth St and Jason Moyo, tel: (14) 706511.

HARARE	J	F	M	A	M	J	J	A	S	O	N	D
AVERAGE TEMP. °F	70	70	68	66	61	57	57	61	66	72	72	70
AVERAGE TEMP. °C	21	21	20	19	16	14	14	16	19	22	22	21
Hours of Sun Daily	7	6	7	8	8	9	9	10	10	9	7	6
RAINFALL ins.	8	8	4	1.5	0.5	0	0	0	0	1.5	4	8
RAINFALL mm	192	181	98	42	10	4	2	3	9	38	94	194
Days of Rainfall	17	15	11	6	2	1	1	1	1	5	11	16

3
Hwange
National Park

Hwange wildlife area (pronounced Hwang-geh, meaning 'peace' in the local Nambia dialect) in the northeast corner of Zimbabwe is the size of East Anglia. From the Zambezi it stretches for 280km (174 miles) halfway to Bulawayo, then across to Botswana and the old hunter–trader Pandamatenga road. It comprises three safari hunting areas, two indigenous forests, the remote **Kazuma Pan National Park,** and in the south, Zimbabwe's premier game reserve and by far its largest: the 14,620km^2 (5645 sq miles) **Hwange National Park**.

A watershed bisects the area, with the Matetse, Deka and Gwayi rivers flowing north to the Zambezi, and deep kalahari sands to the southwest. The coal-mining town **Hwange**, the tourist mecca **Victoria Falls**, and the tiny railway halt of **Dete**, plus the border posts of Pandamatenga and Kazungula, are Hwange's sparse population centres.

Mzilikazi, Zulu-warrior king of the Matabele, invaded the Hwange area in 1828, dispossessing its ruler Hwange Rusambani, and turning the area into his private hunting preserve. Among the early European settlers in the area was German prospector Albert Giese, who heard about the 'stones that burned' from the local people; in 1894 he pegged a claim in what was to be one of the largest coal deposits in the world, thus inducing the routing of the Cape-to-Cairo railway in 1903 via Hwange and the Victoria Falls, rather than Harare–Lake Tanzania direct.

Hwange is still a major producer of coal and continues to fuel the country's large steam locotive fleet.

CLIMATE

November through February are the **summer rain** months in Hwange, bringing life to the grass and water to the pans; it is warm, but not uncomfortable (humidity is seldom a problem in Zimbabwe). The June–July **winter** months are usually **dry** and **sunny**. Hwange can get very cold at this time. A jersey or jacket is essential for nights around the camp-fire.

Opposite: *The game observation tower at the well-patronized Mataka waterhole in Hwange.*

Hwange Town *

Hwange has Wankie Diggers Rugby Club, two-storey shops, banks, and well-watered flowers along Coronation Road. This perky town needs only a coal miner's daughter to seal its fame. There is no Fortnum & Mason, Ultracity or Kirov Ballet, but one of the world's greatest game reserves sits on its shoulder; in fact, Hwange town is the shortest route to Sinamatella Camp situated in the middle of the national park. From Victoria Falls, the nearest camp is Robins, a distance of 110km (68 miles).

Much of Hwange town's affluent 50,000 population works in the power station or on the coal fields. In June 1972, 419 men were killed in an underground explosion in No 2 colliery, where they still lie entombed today.

Dete *

A dusty railway settlement on the northern line, Dete should have been a movie location, but it had to settle for Chibuku breweries, Dete post office, Hi-Lite bakery – and being the phone code for Hwange Main Camp. The village's name means 'a narrow passage', referring perhaps to the twisting terrain the railway navigates nearby, or more likely, the forest-fringed Dete vlei where Victorian adventurer Frederick Selous once hunted. The Game Reserve Hotel offers wild music, *sadza ne nyama* (maize porridge and gravy) and serious drinking. Give then warning and they'll collect you at the station; if you don't, the hotel will be locked up (the trains arrive at impossible midnight hours).

Map showing Hwange National Park, with locations including To Livingstone, Victoria Falls, Matetsi, Hot Spring, Nagapande, Kazuma Pan Nat. Park, Matetsi Safari Area, Hwange, Deka, Lukozi, Gwayi, Bumbusi, Deka Safari Area, Robins, Nantwich, Mandava Pan, Sinamatella Ruins, Dete, To Bulawayo, Deka, Hot Spring, Nyamandhlovu Pan, Main Camp, Hwange National Park, BOTSWANA. Scale: 40 km / 20 miles. N.

Left: *A group of Hwange kudu; this noble-looking antelope is mainly a savannah woodland browser but also feeds on grass.*

HWANGE NATIONAL PARK

Hwange supports 3000 giraffe, 2000 sable, 15,000 buffalo, 6000 impala, 5000 kudu and 3000 zebra. When it was declared a game reserve in 1929, it had been nearly denuded of game by hunters and settlers (it had, in fact, been set aside because it was useless for agriculture). Ted Davison, the first warden, surveyed the reserve and concluded that no rhino existed at all, and there were less than 1000 elephant. Today, latest counts indicate 22,000, the world's most dense population.

The park is divided into three areas or camps: **Main**, **Sinamatella** and **Robins-Nantwich**, with 480km (300 miles) of roads linking them. Eighty per cent of the park (the southern section) is only accessible to specialist camping and photographic safaris. Hwange has at least 413 bird species, 90 varieties of animals, and up to 1000 species of trees and shrubs – of which over 250 have been identified and recorded.

For the historian, the Battle of Hwange (one of the first in Zimbabwe's liberation war) was fought in 1967 between Rhodesian forces and combined ANC (from South Africa) and ZAPU fighters.

Main Camp ★★★

The approach to Main Camp off the main highway at the 'Safari Cross' road junction is a boulevard bordered by park land of giant African trees: Zimbabwe teak 18m (59ft) high, bloodwood, false mopane, camel thorn

---

ON SAFARI

Safari is Swahili for 'walk'. Nowadays not many choose this Dr Livingstone form of exercise; a fully kitted-out land-cruiser is the norm these days. If you don't have your own and you do have the money, let others show you Hwange, under camp-fire canvas or even from a perch in a tree. The list of operators and increasingly luxurious thatched lodges grows daily, but well established in Hwange is **Touch the Wild** with its four Hwange operations, among them the superb Sikumi Tree Lodge, and **Garth Thompson Safari Consultants** in Harare. Hwange Safari Lodge includes pony safaris in its programme.

and the fascinating ordeal tree (*Erythrophleum africanum*), whose poisonous preparations determined an accused's guilt – if he survived the hemlock cup, he was innocent. Local residents regularly walk this route (so do lion).

Main Camp serves as the administrative headquarters and principal entry point for the park. It has a restaurant (The Waterbuck's Head), shop, petrol station and a variety of fully equipped cottages in which overhead fans help to relieve October's heat. Hwange airport lies just outside Main Camp, as does the railway at Dete.

Since Hwange has good underground water reserves, some 60 pans or depressions fed by water pumps were created in the park; these provide the animals with water during the dry winter months, from May to October. Thirty of these occur in the Main Camp area, which has 250km (155 miles) of game-viewing roads.

The **Nyamandhlovu Pan** viewing platform, a short distance from Main Camp, is great for elephant (Nyamandhlovu means 'elephant head' in Sindebele); so is **Gubalala** further on. You may also see giraffe, wildebeest, zebra, baboon, impala and buffalo (in Hwange, some of the herds are up to 1000 strong). To watch a lion kill is rare luck, and leopard are not easily seen. Rhino have been systematically poached for their horns.

Close to Main Camp, the vegetation is savanna and acacia scrub, while 76km (47 miles) along the tar road to **Shumba** picnic area, it is more hilly with mopane and thorn trees. To the southeast, in a 120km loop (75 miles) around the **Manga** and **Kennedy pans**, open grassy vleis or plains spotted with acacia trees prevail.

Southern Hwange is the tip of the Kalahari (which explains the extreme temperature variations; searing midday heat can plummet to exceedingly chilly temperatures in the evenings) and the park may once have been desert. Giant fossil dunes lie in the eastern corner.

Main Camp receives more visitors and cars than elsewhere, but one never sees the bumper-to-bumper Kombi caravans of East Africa, although the Kennedy and Ngwashla pans drive – with 14 safari camps nearby – is fast becoming that way.

Sinamatella ★★

It is a full morning's drive from Main Camp to Sinamatella, past ancient dry riverbeds. Set off early, drive slowly (under 40kph; 25mph) and you should see a good cross-section of Hwange's prolific game – sometimes in vast numbers, and window-winding close. Sinamatella, open year-round, sits on a granite ridge overlooking a valley in fairly thick bush with good mopane forest and generally hillier country than Main Camp. Views stretch for miles in all directions. The Lukosi River loops deep and sandy-dry from Sinamatella into Hwange, as far as **Shumba pans**.

The area has plenty of buffalo; there are crocodile and hippo in **Mandavu Dam**. The national park's facilities at Sinamatella are particularly good – its luxury two-bedroomed cottages overlook the sweeping plains below.

HWANGE RAPTORS
Tawny eagle
Osprey
Wahlberg's eagle
Black sparrowhawk
Booted eagle
Augur buzzard
Ayres' hawk eagle
Yellow-billed kite
African hawk eagle
Peregrine falcon
Martial eagle
Hooded vulture
Brown snake eagle
Dickinson's kestrel
Fish eagle
Chanting goshawk
Bateleur
Gymnogene

Robins Camp ★★

There are probably more lion in the broken country around Robins Camp than anywhere else in the park. Reedbuck and tsessebe antelope seem partial to Robins as well; the tsessebe, brownish purple in colour with its swept-back horns and weighing 140kg (309lb) is

Below: *One of Hwange's few white rhino, target of poachers, joins a bevy of giraffes at the waterhole.*

restricted mainly to the Hwange area, northern Namibia and the northeastern parts of South Africa. Robins has game-viewing hides at **Big Toms** and **Little Toms**, situated on a tributary of the Deka River, and many a twisting road to the pans with names such as **Tsamtsa**, **Tibukai** and **Dandari**. On the Botswana border, near **Jolleys pan**, is a seasonal swamp. East of Robins is a fossil forest and **Manzinchesa hot springs**.

The camp gets its name from Herbert Robins, a recluse and self-taught astronomer whose two farms Little and Big Toms he gave to the nation at his death in 1939. A tall, square tower built for all-night stargazing now forms part of the Robins administration block.

The camp has chalets with outside cooking facilities – watch for incoming lion while you braai!

Nantwich Camp **

Nantwich offers the most remote of the Hwange Park lodges. The check-in point is at Robins Camp and one then drives 11km (7 miles) north. The three two-bedroomed lodges stand well apart from each other on a

bluff overlooking a large vlei (during the rains, a pan). Sit still with a pair of binoculars, and the game will traverse the vlei in casual sequence: wildebeest, bat-eared fox, impala, buffalo, baboon, guinea fowl. And at night, listen to the deliriously chilling whoop of hyena.

Kazuma Pan National Park ***

Similar to the grass plains of East Africa and the great pans of Botswana, with mile after mile of treeless grassland bordered by teak forest, the extremely remote 31,300ha (77,342 acres) Kazuma Pan National Park opened in

1987 in the northwest corner of Zimbabwe. African bush at its most pristine, it is totally different to the rest of Hwange. Only two groups of visitors in four-wheel-drive vehicles are allowed to camp in this wilderness; unfortunately, day visitors are not permitted access.

Great concentrations of game migrate across Kazuma between Botswana and Zimbabwe, especially from September through November, when they make use of the borehole-pumped pans until the rains come. Lion are common and other animals include roan antelope, elephant and buffalo (both in large numbers), gemsbok, giraffe, oribi, zebra and sable. Waterfowl enjoy the pan system in Kazuma, including kingfishers, cormorants, storks and ducks. The rare wattled crane breeds here.

Two primitive water-supplied camp sites, **Insiza** and **Kasetsheti**, provide the only facilities. Wildlife enthusiasts can stay for up to three weeks by booking through National Parks. The park is closed during the months of January and February.

Access to Kazuma National Park is a tough, complicated process as it is via the old Pandamatenga–Hunters road, now the Zimbabwe–Botswana border. Obtain full details when booking, or from the warden at Matetsi where one checks in, 25km (16 miles) off the Victoria Falls road. Access from Kazungula is tempting but not permitted. Tour operator Backpackers Africa at Victoria Falls offers a three-day walking safari into Kazuma.

Opposite: *A roan, among the rarer of the antelopes.*
Top: *Elephant in Hwange.*

HUNTERS' DOMAIN

Half of Zimbabwe's park and wildlife area is set aside for safari hunting, which is undoubtedly unsettling news to anti-blood sport readers. The theory, however, is that the high hunting-trophy fees guarantee the survival of the habitat, the animals who occupy it, and provide an income for peasant communal-area residents on whose land some hunting takes place. The animals' opinions have to date not been sourced. The exercise is controlled by National Parks ecologists who set animal quotas; there are 35 species that can be hunted. The standards of professional hunters are policed through the Safari Operators Association and the Professional Hunters Association.

Deka and Matetsi Safari Areas **

Mopane woodland broken up by sandy ridges with scrubby commiphora and combretum woodland marks **Deka**'s 51,000ha sport-hunting area (126,020 acres). It lies between the town of Hwange and Sinamatella Camp in the north of Hwange National Park. There are no facilities, and hunters, who do experience competition from poachers, have to rely on the iced water in the cool boxes of their four-wheel-drives.

The Panda-Masui forest and Kazuma Pan separate the two halves of the **Matetsi Hunting and Safari Area** beyond Hwange National Park, in the northwest of Zimbabwe. This region of nearly 300,000ha (741,300 acres) used to be farmed, but because of erratic rainfall and poor soils it was abandoned. The smaller of the two areas adjoins the Zambezi River and stretches for 30km (19 miles) from the multination border post at Kazungula to the Zambezi National Park; the larger, southerly section forms Hwange Park's northern border. Woodlands of teak and mukwa (bloodwood) grow on the kalahari sands area, while mopane scrub and woodland flourish on the karoo basalt soils that feature in 25% of the region. Matetsi is well renowned for its hunting – of sable (the animal is particularly prolific in this area), as well as all other game (elephant, buffalo, eland, roan). Considerable research into game ranching has been undertaken here.

The tiny village of Matetsi itself (named after the river) lies on the railway line some 60km (35 miles) south of Victoria Falls. The warden's office, the entry point for the Matetsi Safari Area and Kazuma Pan, is 10km (6 miles) further on. Nearby is the Matetsi River Ranch which has its own airstrip.

Below: *The private Jabulisa lodge, outside Hwange park.*

Hwange National Park at a Glance

BEST TIMES TO VISIT

The best time is during the winter from **May to October**, when the grass is thin, and the animals congregate at the pans. Most of the park's accommodation facilities are open year-round, but some game-viewing roads, particularly in the Robins, Nantwich and Deka camp areas, are closed November to April.

GETTING THERE

Air Zimbabwe operates **daily flights** to Hwange from Harare and Victoria Falls, tel: (118) 393; unlicensed airstrip at Main Camp for private aircraft. Other options are: **by car** from Bulawayo to Main Camp; **by rail** to Dete Station; by **rural bus** from Bulawayo or Victoria Falls.

GETTING AROUND

Use **own transport**, join a **UTC bus tour** or make use of Hwange Safari Lodge **Land-Rovers**. Hitchhiking is not allowed. **Car-hire** facilities at Hwange Safari Lodge, call Hertz, tel: (118) 393.

WHERE TO STAY

Gwaai River Hotel, 34km (21 miles) from Main Camp: an eccentric Africa version of 'Fawlty Towers', hunters' haunt, offers good value, tel: (118) 355.

Private safari lodges
Hwange Safari Lodge, 12km (7 miles) from Main Camp: overlooks elephant

pan, centre for safari operators, call Zimbabwe Sun, tel: (14) 736644.
Sikumi Tree Lodge (thatched tree-top units) and **Makololo Tent Camp**: luxury in the wilderness, call Touch the Wild Safaris, tel: (19) 74589.
Detema Safari Lodge: promises the 'big five', tel: (14) 735995.
Sable Valley Lodge: Queen Elizabeth and the Duke of Edinburgh stayed here in 1991, tel: (19) 74589.
Kanondo Tree Camp: presidential elephant herd resident nearby, tel: (118) 273.
Ivory Lodge: tree-houses overlooking waterhole, tel: (118) 3402.
Matetsi River Ranch: big-game hunting, tel: (113) 433525.

BUDGET ACCOMMODATION
National Parks self-catering chalets: at Main Camp, Robins and Nantwich, as well as at Bumbusi, Lukosi (both near Sinamatella) and Deka Exclusive (parties to a maximum of 12); also **camping and caravan sites**, call National Parks central booking office, tel: (14) 706077.
Game Reserve Hotel, Dete: rustic, tel: (118) 366.

WHERE TO EAT

The Baobab is the best restaurant in Hwange town, tel: (181) 2323.
Main Camp and **Sinamatella** have restaurants and bars, while all of Hwange's **safari lodges** offer excellent meals. A limited range of foodstuffs can be purchased at the Main and Sinamatella camps' stores, but visitors should come fully provisioned.

TOURS AND EXCURSIONS

Bush walks: accompanied by armed ranger; also full-moon night walks, call National Parks, tel: (118) 371.
Walking safaris in Hwange: try Touch the Wild, tel: (19) 74589.
Game drives: arrange at any safari lodge.
Photographic safaris: Ivory Safaris, tel: (118) 3402.

USEFUL TELEPHONE NUMBERS

Backpackers Africa, tel: (113) 4471.
Garth Thompson Safari Consultants, tel: (14) 795202.
National Parks central booking office, tel: (14) 706077.
Touch the Wild Safaris, tel: (19) 74589.
United Touring Company (UTC), tel: (118) 393.

HWANGE	J	F	M	A	M	J	J	A	S	O	N	D
AVERAGE TEMP. °F	75	73	73	70	63	57	59	63	72	75	77	75
AVERAGE TEMP. °C	24	23	23	2	17	14	15	17	22	24	25	24
Hours of Sun Daily	8	8	8	9	9	9	10	11	11	9	9	7
RAINFALL ins.	6	5	3	1.5	0	0	0	0	0	1	2	6
RAINFALL mm	162	147	72	32	4	1	0	1	4	24	67	155
Days of Rainfall	16	14	9	4	1	0	0	0	1	4	10	15

4
Victoria Falls

Standing at the main falls, with the chasm at one's feet and the rain forest at one's back, a horizon-to-horizon cavalry charge of water and spray surges 60m (66yd) away: this is the **Victoria Falls**, a World Heritage Site. The first European recordings of these falls were made by Scottish missionary David Livingstone, who was so moved at his sighting of the magnificent waters, that his famous, much-quoted words are now familiar to most.

Shongwe was the name the Tokaleya people, who still live there, gave the falls. Mzilikazi's wandering Zulu-Ndebele referred to them as *amanza thunquayo* or 'water rising as smoke', while the Kololo, on the run from other marauding *impis*, called them *mosi oa tunya* (the one we use today): 'smoke that thunders'.

California's Bridal Veils Falls is the world's largest, Angel Falls in Venezuela the highest, Khone in Laos the widest; but what makes Victoria Falls different is that its immense curtain of water is so visible, a total experience. As an attraction, it is high on Africa's 'don't miss' list.

The Victoria Falls area, in Zimbabwe's northwestern corner, stretches from Kazungula where Zambia, Botswana, Namibia and Zimbabwe meet, back along 60km (37 miles) of the **Zambezi River** to the falls, and then for 130km (80 miles) down the mountain-hemmed **Batoka gorge** and **Devil's Cataract** to where the river opens out into Lake Kariba. To the south is Hwange Game Reserve; to the north, the 1905 Edwardian bridge links Zambia with Zimbabwe. There are two national parks in the area, and the town of Victoria Falls itself.

CLIMATE

On the banks of the Zambezi, the weather is **exceptionally hot** for most of the year. In **winter** (June and July) the days are **warm**, but cool at night. November brings the rain; at this time, and the weeks preceding it, air conditioning is a boon as even the nights can be hot, humid and tropical. Victoria Falls lies at an altitude of 880m (2887ft), twice as high as Lake Kariba downstream.

Opposite: *Bird's-eye view of the Victoria Falls and its spectacular gorge.*

DON'T MISS

*** Devil's Cataract and a walk through the rain forest
*** White-water rafting
*** A walking safari with knowledgeable rangers
*** The annual Zambezi River Festival; world white-water rafting championships
** Africa Spectacular dancing at Falls Craft Village or Victoria Falls Hotel; dinner in the Livingstone Room
** Small-boat game-viewing on the Zambezi
** A walk across the bridge to Zambia's Eastern Cataract
** A drive through the river-side Zambezi National Park; lovely picnic and fishing spots.

Victoria Falls Village *

Victoria Falls, surprisingly still a village, is set 1km (half a mile) back from the falls and consists of two main roads: Livingstone Way, a continuation of the Bulawayo and airport road that runs past the falls and over the bridge, and Parkway, branching off Livingstone at Publicity Association corner, and running past hill-perched residences and hotels to the Zambezi National Park entrance gate. This tourist spot of 12,000 people is a conglomeration of hotels, curio shops, a craft village, and Chinotimba township. It also features a railway that cuts the village in two, safari operators, backpackers in rafter sandals and Zambian matrons hurrying to the border post alongside pushcarts loaded with foodstuffs.

Direct flights connect Victoria Falls with Bulawayo, Harare, Johannesburg, and Namibia.

Spencer's Creek Crocodile Ranch *

The crocodile ranch, 5km (3 miles) from town along Parkway, has outgrown its rough-and-ready act and is now the elegant **Zambezi Nature Sanctuary** with its eco-logically correct natural history museum, video auditorium, quiet shop, cool leafy walkways, tea gardens, streams, greenery and wooden bridges. There is also an open-air 'vulture restaurant' where members of this protected species can be watched while feeding. The ranch has 10,000 Nile crocodiles. Eggs are collected in the wild and the ranch then restocks the depleted Zambezi with young crocodiles, who in fact help to balance the fish popula-tion by preying on bream-eating predators. Crocodile skin is exceptionally elegant but before purchasing, check whether your country allows noncattle leathers.

VICTORIA FALLS NATIONAL PARK

This park surrounds and protects the falls. Upstream of the surging waters, it stretches past David Livingstone's oft-photographed statue; downstream it nestles between the railway line and the zigzag gorges of the Zambezi, thus managing to keep man, habitation and hotel chains at bay.

Above: *Devil's Cataract and its familiar rainbow. The spray, which at peak flow rises to a cloud discernible from a considerable distance, nurtures an enchanting rain forest.*

The 'rain forest' at the falls is actually a normal riverine forest, yet quite lovely: lianas, blood lilies, orchids, ferns, small buck, monkeys and sunbirds share space in this jungle of mahogany, fig, sausage tree and ebony. Spray-intoxicated and watched over by Dr Livingstone's angels, this little forest is the constant companion of the falls' thunder symphony.

Admission to the park is along Livingstone Way, opposite the carpark (and water-ice sellers), 200m (219yd) from the border post; go through the thatched National Parks display.

The Victoria Falls ★★★

A surge of green-white water compressed into the gap between the bank on which one stands and Cataract Island forms **Devil's Cataract**, the first fall. It is an awesome roaring, earth-trembling fury of beauty and power right at one's feet, with only carefully placed thorn bush dividing the view from eternity. Behind is **Livingstone's statue** – huge, bronzed, purposeful – gazing over the waterfall he made known to the Western world and offered to his Queen on 16 November 1855. Devil's Cataract shrinks considerably in the dry season, exposing a flat platform of black basalt. Upriver, facing the

---

FACTS ON THE FALLS

• At Victoria Falls, the Zambezi is 1000km (621 miles) from its source.
• In length the falls are 1708m (5604ft).
• The average height of the falls is 100m (328ft).
• In November, 20,000m³ (706,300 cu ft) per minute goes over the falls, but it has been known to reach 500,000m³ (17.6 million cu ft) per minute.

Below: *African tribal costume and dance at the falls – a vibrant spectacle. All of Zimbabwe's ethnic groups are represented at the Craft Village.*

cataract and rain forest, is a good spot at full moon to see the lunar rainbow etched in the spray and rising from the depths of the chasm. There is a path down the side of the cataract to a viewing platform with the waterfall to the left, the churning gorge ahead, a dripping rock face, billows of spray, rainbows, and jungle all around.

To see the **Main Falls**, the light is best in the early morning or late afternoon. The spray – like gusts of rain in sunlight – makes a raincoat, hat and plastic camera bag essential, particularly during the maximum-flow period from April to June. The path at the lip of the falls meanders from Devil's Cataract through the rain forest, and then out into rainbowed sunlight and updrafts of spray at ever more exotic viewpoints over the chasm. As one weaves in and out of the forest to the next view site, it is alive with birds, butterflies and small forest creatures. Sit on a rustic bench and enjoy. A tip: take no pictures first time through; do that on the return leg.

The sequence of the falls begins with Devil's Cataract, then follow the Main Falls, **Livingstone Island** (where Kololo canoemen escorted the explorer), **Horseshoe Falls**, **Rainbow Falls**, and finally **Danger Point**, which overlooks the **Boiling Pot**, Zambia and the river's escape route to the next of many zigzagging gorges.

At Danger Point, the forest peters out through wispy weaver-nested palms to an open rocky platform. Be careful when approaching the slippery edge; no-one has come back from a trip down.

The return route runs closer to the bridge with its main-arch span of 152m (500ft); it carries one rail and one road track.

Recently, a New Zealand–South African company has established a bungee-jumping concern for those who enjoy the thrill of death-defying leaps into the gorge.

Left: *Entrance to the venerable Edwardian-colonial Victoria Falls Hotel, whose hospitable doors have been admitting guests since the first years of the century.*

Victoria Falls Hotel *

This chunky, orange-tiled hotel with its courtyard, patios, colonnades, huge trees and views over the falls and bridge is pure raj. Built in 1904 and refurbished many times, its white-gloved atmosphere and superb setting rival Singapore's Raffles, Bombay's Taj Mahal and Cape Town's Mount Nelson. At the entrance, a short treed walk from the Edwardian railway station, hangs a Victorian filigreed name-sign, a memento from a Sherlock Holmes film.

Some may opt for the **Makishi folk dancing** or the marimbas on the patio, but should one prefer the elegant nostalgia of a more gracious era, book a table in the **Livingstone Room**, the hotel's main dining room. Here, the *Mandebvu* (meaning 'beards') quartet plays reprises from the fifties, as well as their own jazz compositions.

The walk from the hotel to the falls in Edwardian days consisted of being carried in a ricksha; today the walk leads you through a parkland of lawns and huge trees past the **Makasa Sun Casino Hotel**.

Zambian Bank **

The **Eastern Cataract**, a dozen rushing streams among the palms before the final leap over the basalt brink, is definitely worth a visit. It is only a walk or a bicycle ride through Immigration and across the bridge. The knife

---

DAVID LIVINGSTONE

Livingstone, the Scots-born missionary explorer who discovered Victoria Falls for the English-speaking world, has been castigated for being selfish and stubborn, for mistrusting his colleagues and being hard on his family. But what he did is the stuff of legend: the first European to cross Africa coast to coast, he inspired a generation. Livingstone did much to end the ravages of the slave trade, and he was persistent in his almost mystical pursuit of the source of the Nile. Found dead, kneeling in prayer by his camp cot, two of his workers carried his body to the coast to be later buried in Westminster Abbey. His wife, Mary, had died earlier in Mozambique.

Above: A bungee-jumper braves the plunge into a gorge at Victoria Falls.
Opposite: Basket-weaving at the Craft Village.

edge is spray-filled and deafening – a must to visit. Canoes sometimes gather at the **Boiling Pot**. You can also bargain for malachite brace-lets at the craft market.

The Zambezi River ★★★

The Zambezi, 2700km (1678 miles) long, is wide and shallow above the falls. The best way to see it is not on a sundowner cruise but in a small outboard-driven pon-toon which glides along the banks for superb game-viewing. With a storm coming on, the high ilala palms, snorting hippo and tangled riverine jungle give it a primeval heart-of-darkness edge. At **Kandahar Island** 10km (6 miles) upstream, the river reveals islands and rapids (no Kololo in dugout canoes, these days).

But the real adventure is the three-day white-water canoeing trail along a 65km (40 miles) stretch of the river, starting at Kazungula, proceeding downstream through the Katombora and Sansimba rapids and ending at the Big Tree, Victoria Falls. This is the real Africa: small groups of people led by expert guides, two-man klepper canoes gliding silently beneath the waterberry trees and tented camps on the river bank at night.

White-water Rafting ★★★

This attraction has transformed the falls in the last 10 years. Young and not-so-young come from all over to experience the world's wildest one-day white-water run.

It was started by Sobec, an American company still operating on the Zambian side. In Zimbabwe there are several operators, among them Shearwater, the most experienced, and Frontiers. The 22km (14 miles) run through 19 gorges, some only 12m (39ft) wide with 400m (1312ft) cliffs to the left and right, is exhilarating big-river action. The inflatable Avon rubber-rafts bounce and twist in the surging water and spray, navigated by a daredevil skilled oarsman and seven passengers who shift their body weight to manoeuvre the bucking craft. Several rafts do the run together, thus helping each other.

The rafting only operates during the months of July through mid-March. Those who have done it will tell you at the Explorers pub that nothing can beat the 24km low-water option (15 miles) from mid-August to December. This counts as a grade-five run (rapids are graded one to six); six is nonrunnable.

Zambezi National Park **

The National Parks lodges here, 6km (4 miles) from the village, afford secluded frontage on the banks of the Zambezi. Warthog snuffle, hippo snort and, in the high-tufted ilala palms, African fish eagle cry as sundowner cruise ships float gently by.

The park, 57,000ha (140,847 acres), stretches west to the **Matetsi Safari Area** and south for 24km (15 miles). It is known for fine herds of sable and practically every other animal, among them, elephant, lion, zebra and waterbuck. The viewing, though, is not as good as in Hwange. The Zambezi circular drive flanks the river with its rapids and huge overhanging fig, ebony, and apple-ring acacias with their elegant pods. One oddity is a sealed-off minefield on the river bank, a relic of the liberation war 15 years ago. There are several fishing camps, and half-day foot safaris through the park, accompanied by armed guides, are also available.

GONE FISHING

Three National Parks fishing camps on the Zambezi riverbank upstream of the falls offer bream (using worms) and fighting tigerfish (using trace and lure). They are **Kandahar** (open year-round), **Mpala-Jana** and **Sansimba**; four more have recently been added. Boats can be hired; the shelters are basic but have toilets and showers. The waters are international so no licences are needed. Reasonably wild and remote, these camps are not for those who wake at every sound.

Further inland, the vegetation is more open savannah and mopane woodland. The Chamabondo drive south from the town on the main highway leads to the **Kaliankua pan** game-viewing hide and the game-viewing platform at **Njoko pan**. The Kazungula road runs right through the middle of the park to the Botswana border.

Victoria Falls at a Glance

BEST TIMES TO VISIT

All year round; the falls are magical throughout the seasons, but their flow is lowest in November and December, hence less spectacular. The end of the rains from **February** and **March** onwards see the heaviest flow and volume of spray. The area is always warm.

GETTING THERE

Visitors can fly to **Victoria Falls airport** from Kariba, Hwange, Harare, Bulawayo, Johannesburg, Gaborone and Windhoek; call Air Zimbabwe, tel: (113) 4316, or (14) 575021. (Airport passenger handling, under the pressure of Vic Falls tourism, can lack a confident, caring touch.) Tourists can also arrive by **train** (including steam train) from Bulawayo and Zambia; or by **tar road** from Harare, Beitbridge, Bulawayo and Lusaka. There are good gravel roads from Namibia and Botswana entering at Kazungula, and a 50% gravel road along Harare's scenic route via Karoi to Hwange. **Rural buses** to Victoria Falls leave from Bulawayo. The most interesting route is by car to Kariba, then **overnight car ferry** to Mlibizi at the headwaters of Lake Kariba – two hours from the falls.

GETTING AROUND

On foot is best, or by **hired bicycle**; the village is small. Hail a **taxi**, **hire a car**

(Europcar, tel: (113) 4344; Avis, tel: (113) 4532; Hertz, tel: (113) 4267), or catch a **UTC** or **hotel bus**. You can also join a four-wheel-drive safari; check at any hotel for details on the above. Other options are **scooter hire**, tel: (113) 4402, or a Vic Falls Rambler (a tractor-pulled trailer).

WHERE TO STAY

National Parks lodges and nine, mainly exclusive, game-viewing and fishing camps: write well in advance to National Parks, PO Box 8365, Causeway, Harare; tel: (14) 706077, or call Victoria Falls, tel: (113) 4222.
Victoria Falls Hotel: the original hotel, this white and pink dowager princess overlooks the Victoria Falls bridge; colonial, lush setting of trees and lawns, patio dining, call the Zimbabwe Sun group, tel: (113) 4203.
Elephant Hills: enormous 'Aztec city of the sun' conference hotel with 18-hole golf course and panoramic views of the Zambezi River, call the Zimbabwe Sun group, tel: (113) 4793.
The Lodge at Victoria Falls: opened December 1994, large 72-roomed thatched hotel overlooking Zambezi National Park, faces sunset rather than river, tel: (14) 708737.
Rainbow Hotel: good mid-range choice, arched Arabic architecture overlooking a rain forest of trees, tel: (113) 4585.

A'Zambezi: double-storey thatched semicircular lodge at riverside location, quiet, good for bird-watching, warthog roam on lawns by the pool, tel: (113) 4561.
Ilala Lodge: centrally situated, huge thatched complex, video venue for river rafters, also has disco nightclub, call the Zimbabwe Sun group, tel: (113) 4737.
Makasa Sun Casino: most attractive pool in town, lovely open-air breakfast boma, tel: (113) 4275.
Sprayview Hotel: recently refurbished, owner-run, safari-operators' favourite (though they tend to be fickle), tel: (113) 4344.
Victoria Falls Safari Lodge (self-catering): not cheap, but nice thatched two-bedroomed units, tel: (113) 4714.
Masuwe Safari Lodge: safari tents on platform stilts overlooking pool and Zambezi River, tel: (113) 426512.
Westwood Game Lodge, 40 minutes from the falls: beneath river-bank trees, tel: (113) 4614.
Imbabala Safari Camp: eight en-suite chalets on Zambezi, near Kazungula and Caprivi, tel: (113) 4219.

BUDGET ACCOMMODATION
Homestead Affordable Accommodation: also offers canoeing, tel: (113) 4773.
Town Council Rest Camp: offers camping, caravanning and also chalets; cheap, tel: (113) 4210.

Victoria Falls at a Glance

WHERE TO EAT

All hotels have one or more restaurants with an à la carte menu.

Livingstone Room, Victoria Falls Hotel: elegant dining, hotel also offers evening patio buffet-braai, tel: (113) 4203.

The Pizza Bistro, Sopers Cntr: crêpes, pasta and pizzas; small, homely, good food, tel: (113) 4396.

Explorers, Sopers Cntr: river rafters' rave-up spot, pub food, wild music; no rafter under 25 would be seen anywhere else, tel: (113) 4298.

Boma Restaurant, Victoria Falls Safari Lodge: open-air game meat and *potjiekos* (many-layered stew cooked in black three-legged pot), re-commended, tel: (113) 4725.

The Cattleman, Phumula Mall: new, clean steakhouse, tel: (113) 4767.

Naran's Takeaways, Sopers Cntr: Indian food, tel: (113) 4425.

TOURS AND EXCURSIONS

Bird-watching safaris: contact Mwari Komborera/ Bonaventure Cruises, tel: (113) 4243.

Bungee-jumping (off Victoria Falls bridge): call Kiwi Extreme, Livingstone, Zambia, tel: (260-3) 321806, or book at the bridge.

Canoeing, upper Zambezi: call Shearwater Adventures, tel: (113) 4471, or Zambezi Canoe, tel: (113) 4298.

Flight of Angels: for small aircraft and helicopters, call

United Air, tel: (113) 4530, or Southern Cross Aviation, tel: (113) 4618; for microlite, call Batoka Sky (operates from Zambia), tel: (113) 4424.

Game-viewing safaris: all Vic Falls operators offer game drives; try Wilderness Safaris, tel: (113) 4527, or Safari Travel Agency, tel: (113) 4571; for night drives, tel: (113) 4614.

Horse trails: call Shearwater Adventures, tel: (113) 4471.

Hunting safaris: call Um-kombo Safaris, tel: (113) 4453 (an 18-day elephant hunt will cost US$15,000 per person, plus an extra US$8000 for the elephant).

River cruising: ask for a small craft; call Kalambeza Safaris, tel: (113) 4480; Frontiers, tel: (113) 4772; Dabula Safaris, tel: (113) 4453.

Sundowner cruises on Zambezi: many Vic Falls com-panies offer these boat trips, known as 'booze cruises'; try Zambezi Wilderness Safaris, tel: (113) 4637, or UTC, tel: (113) 4267.

Walking safaris: Back-packers Africa, tel: (113) 4510 or 4424; also Dabula Safaris, tel: (113) 4453.

White-water rafting: Shearwater, tel: (113) 4471; Frontiers, tel: (113) 4772.

Zambia adventure options: Safari Par Excellence, tel: (113) 4510 or (14) 750485; day trips (include Livingstone Museum), call Kubu Cabins, tel: (113) 4714.

SAFARI OPERATORS

Abercrombie and Kent Safaris: big international operator, tel: (113) 4780.

Dabula Safaris: reservations for Zambezi River Camp, tel: (113) 4453.

Game Trackers (southern Africa): tel: (113) 4381.

Shearwater Adventures: white-water rafting, canoeing, walking safaris, horse trails, tel: (113) 4648 or 4471.

Touch the Wild: meet-the-people cultural expeditions a speciality, tel: (113) 4676.

United Touring Company (**UTC**): touring and excursions, tel: (113) 4267.

USEFUL TELEPHONE NUMBERS

Bicycle Hire, Bushtrackers, tel: (113) 4348, or ask at Sprayview Hotel.

National Parks (Victoria Falls), Livingstone Way, tel: (113) 4222 or 4210.

Victoria Falls Publicity Association, cnr Parkway and Livingstone Way, tel: (113) 4202.

VICTORIA FALLS	J	F	M	A	M	J	J	A	S	O	N	D
AVERAGE TEMP. °F	75	75	82	70	64	59	59	64	72	77	77	75
AVERAGE TEMP. °C	24	24	28	21	18	15	15	18	22	25	25	24
Hours of Sun Daily	7	7	8	9	10	10	10	10	10	9	7	7
RAINFALL ins.	5	5	3	1	0	0	0	0	0	3	3	5
RAINFALL mm	125	138	71	23	2	1	0	1	2	24	77	138
Days of Rainfall	14	13	7	3	1	0	0	0	1	3	10	14

5
Lake Kariba

Kariba is an inland sea, 282km (175 miles) long, cre-ated by a dam built across the Zambezi River. Completed in 1958, it is Africa's third-largest dam and forms the country's major source of hydroelectric power. More than a million cubic metres of concrete were used for the massive dam wall, and around 80 people lost their lives during its construction.

Lake Kariba is a wilderness of water, big game and baobab islands; its shores, particularly those of the **Matusadona** and **Chizarira national parks**, are rich in elephant, buffalo and crocodile – and you're never out of earshot of the fish eagle. It has become a very popular recreational area for Zimbabweans, and some of the country's finest game lodges and water-sport facilities (including yachting and fishing) are to be found here.

The village of Kariba has tourist hotels, an airport, Zimbabwe's main hydroelectric power station, and up at Kariba Heights, **Santa Barbara**'s circular church which was built to commemorate the Italians who lived and died during the construction of the dam.

There is a touch of Hemingway in fishing villages such as Kariba: people don't mess around with boats here – they abandon loved ones for them! Commercial fishing based on *kapenta* (Lake Tanzania sardine) is important, sport fishing is very popular. To service both industries there are marinas, boat yards, salvagers, anchorages – and Andora harbour, from where all vessels set forth.

Visitors to Zimbabwe normally combine Kariba, Hwange and the Victoria Falls in one trip.

CLIMATE

Kariba experiences the **high-est temperatures** of all Zimbabwe's wilderness areas: in November 1955, the mer-cury soared to 46°C (115°F), and it often hovers in the 40s in the months of October through February. Ice, air conditioning and showers are part of Kariba's lifestyle. On the lake, the sun scorches; but it can also be cool at night, particularly in June and July. **November to February** the **rains** fall, and the storms on the lake are wondrous.

Opposite: *Kariba's dam wall with Nyaminyami, river god of the Zambezi, in the foreground.*

DON'T MISS

*** Kariba Ferry to Mlibizi
*** A few days on a
Matusadona safari island
*** Bird- and game-
watching from a small boat
(bring binoculars)
*** A walking trail in the
supremely remote Chizarira
National Park
** A boat trip up Sanyati
Gorge
** Trolling for tigerfish
* A visit to Kariba's dam wall
* Santa Barbara Church and
Operation Noah monument
* Sundowners at the Lake
View Inn
* Crocodile tails for dinner
* Buy a carved Nyaminyami
walking stick.

LAKE KARIBA

When Kariba was built, 50,000 Gwembe Tonga became exiles, translocated from their Zambezi river shores. That was the worst effect when 1,000,000 cubic metres (35.3 million cu ft) of concrete and 10,000 tonnes of reinforced steel were dumped across the Kariba gorge. The other effect was the plight of the animals: over 5000 sq km (1930 sq miles) of bush was inundated and thousands were trapped by the rising waters. Thousands of others were rescued by conservationist Rupert Fothergill in the quixotic Operation Noah.

The Zambezi continues to run beneath the lake, and the flora and fauna haven't changed much since the flooding. Kariba weed (*Salvinia auriculata*) with its great floating mats was for a time a threat, and torpedo grass (*Panicum repens*) on the shoreline has become dry-season grazing for buffalo and elephant. The lake's pinks and mauves at sunset on the Matusadona mountains contrast with ghostly drowned trees shimmering in their reflections, and providing perches for cormorants, kingfishers,

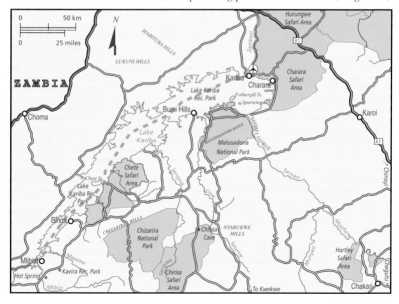

darters and herons. Beneath the waters are 42 species of fish and jellyfish, sponges and mussels.

Matusadona National Park ***

Matusadona means 'the constant dripping of dung'. On the southern shore of Lake Kariba, directly opposite the village 25km (16 miles) distant, the park can be divided into drowned tree-top lake shore with its browsing buffalo, then, on the plain, mopane woodland and tangled jesse bush favoured by elephant and rhino, and finally, the sudden upward thrust of the Matusadona mountains and escarpment.

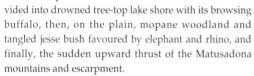

Above: *An aerial view of Lake Kariba and its attractive Caribbea Bay resort and small craft harbour.*

Matusadona is the home of Kariba's luxury safari camps, thatched or tented resorts offering every form of game, boat and walking trail. And there are fully equipped National Parks camps, some with chalets. The one at Muuyu (meaning baobab), surrounded by a low-walled boma, looks out across a grassed lake shore teeming with impala. Returning from a fishing trip, you can be hemmed in by hippo near the mooring tree, grazing buffalo in front of the camp, and elephant coming down to drink. Access is usually by boat from Kariba, often by light aircraft. By road, it is 300km (186 miles) of bone-jarring adventure; a four-wheel-drive vehicle is advisable.

Safari Style ***

Bumi Hills is the most luxurious of the lodges, set high on a bluff west of Matusadona National Park. The Wild Bunch don't frequent Bumi, the Well-Heeled do. It has beautifully cool rooms with a poolside dining area surrounded by frangipani and bougainvillea for elegant elephant viewing. Its sister resort, a series of wooden houseboats up the Chiuri River nearby, is uniquely wild.

KARIBA DAM

The concrete-arch wall is 579m (1900ft) long and 128m (420ft) high. The rock at the foot of the outer wall has been scoured out by 60m (197ft) by the force of the water through the six escape gates. At its base the dam is 24m (79ft) thick – longer than a cricket pitch. The dam was opened by the Queen Mother on 17 May 1960.

You can walk onto the dam wall and feel the throb of the great underground turbines. The best view is at the Publicity Bureau, 1km (half a mile) up a winding road from the Shell Station.

Sanyati Lodge, hidden in the trees on a rocky lake cliff, is an exclusive little resort on the edge of the Sanyati gorge. It is particularly good for painting and bird-watching. The deep, mountainous, forested, and rather eerie gorge is the eldorado of Zimbabwean fishermen.

Spurwing Island, with its tents under thatch, has a two-storey pub, also thatched, overlooking lake and mountain. The evening meal is heralded by drums.

Fothergill Island, named after the ranger, has its own airstrip which has to be cleared first of impala before landing can take place. Tiny electric guard-wires ensure prowling lion don't encamp on your chalet verandah!

Tiger Bay features possibly the best chalet units of all the resorts in a lovely setting of grassy slopes and mango trees on the Ume River. Serious fishermen prefer this resort, so with the din of their 200HP outboard motors, forget about late lie-ins.

Chizarira National Park **

Chizarira, perched on the Zambezi escarpment with its magnificent mountains, is the most remote of Zimbabwe's national parks and difficult to access. It is set 50km (31 miles) inland from Lake Kariba, a wilderness of mountain, river gorge, flood plain and plateau. Its name comes from the Tonga word 'barrier'. The highest mountain is Tundazi, above the Zambezi valley, supposedly the home of a huge and powerful serpent.

National Parks operate six exclusive camps in Chizarira, together with armed backpacking wilderness trails and daytime walks. Backpackers Africa operate five-day trails. The park has a population of 1000 elephant; Chizarira's good water supply also attracts tsessebe, buffalo, roan, sable and zebra. Black rhino are continually being poached.

With its escarpment-sliced gorges such as **Mucheni** and **Mamvuri**, and long-distance views over the Zambezi valley, Chizarira is for the real wilderness *aficionado*, not the big-five collector. From sunrise to sunset you will see no-one and hear nothing but the sounds of the bush: bird, predator and other creatures of the wild. The **Chizarira Wilderness Safari Lodge** is surrounded by pristine wilderness and its chalets perch dramatically at the edge of the cliff; it also has a swimming pool.

The park has a gravel airstrip. From Victoria Falls by road the distance is 300km (186 miles); a four-wheel-drive vehicle is necessary.

CHIZARIRA WILDERNESS TRAILS

Chizarira is the finest wilderness area for backpacking in Zimbabwe. Trails are conducted during the dry season by armed **National Parks** wardens and by **Backpackers Africa** or **Shearwater Adventures** year-round. Backpackers have two trails, the Lwizilukulu gorge and the Busi flood plain on the park's southern edge, for a minimum of four walkers and five days. Two-man tents and all equipment are supplied; hikers are taken to Chizarira in a four-wheel-drive from Victoria Falls. Sijarira Forest on the lake shore is also a hiking area.

Opposite: *Visitors take to the lake's waters around Spurwing Island, which is large enough to support its own big-game population.*
Left: *Scanning the horizons at Chizarira park on the Zambezi escarpment.*

Houseboating Paradise ★★★

Kariba offers mountain, lake, big game, and bird-watching. Your enjoyment will be enhanced if you fish, or enjoy sea cruises. Locals trail their own boats, everything can be hired, however.

Sundowner trips run by **United Touring Company** (UTC) are for those who like to sip as the sun sets, while **Cruise Kariba** offers full-day game-viewing to the Matusadona islands. Or you can hire a luxury cruiser plus skipper from the **Kariba Breezes marina**. Boats can be hired by the hour or a whole ferry from **DDF** (District Development Fund, a government-run shipping services ferry). You can also rent a yacht that sleeps up to four from **Kariba Yachts** at the Cutty Sark marina; or best of all, one of **Sail Safaris**' luxurious six-day safaris on a Tiki 30 catamaran.

A weekend on a houseboat is often a perk for the Zimbabwe executive. The excuse is fishing, but is more likely to be Chardonnay sipping …

Houseboats come in all boat-builder's shapes and home-made varieties. They can be six-berth cabin cruisers or huge paddle-wheel, multideck Mississippi monsters. You will see them mid-lake or parked among the dead trees off the Matusadona islands. Cruise guests swim in mid-lake to avoid shoreline bilharzia and crocodiles (a fallacy, since they cruise the deep waters as well). Be aware of the unpredictable violent storms that can blow up suddenly on Kariba's waters.

AFRICAN QUEEN

Cruising a great African lake on an overnight journey of 282km (175 miles) can only be romantic; but there are no private cabins, black tie for dinner or big swing band. The **Kariba Ferry** is rather like an enormous picnic with passengers lazing on reclining chairs on the covered deck, a sun lounge above and the cars below. The meals are no huge, and come nightfall, the crew bring out palliasses. Highlights before reaching journey's end at **Mlibizi** are a croc-defying dive off the deck, an absurdly beautiful sunset and game spotting by torchlight in the Chete narrows.

There are numerous marinas at Kariba with their flotillas of pleasure craft tucked in behind horseshoe-shaped barriers. Nearly all the hotels have one nestling in the water below their verandahs – they form the usual pick-up points for Kariba island-safaris.

Kariba, Haunt of Fishermen **

The tigerfish is a bony, razor-toothed fighting fish, weighing 3kg (7lb) on average, but it can weigh as much as 15kg (33lb). Silver with black stripes, and flashes of orange on its fins, it is prone to sudden surges and water-clearing leaps. This 'striped water dog' is voraciously carnivorous, patrolling in both deep and shallow waters, taking *kapenta* or spinner. In October an annual international tigerfishing competition is held at Kariba.

There are 22 species of bream in Zimbabwe, as well as carp and black bass, among others, and the shallow waters along the jigsaw-puzzle shore of Matusadona are well supplied. Aspirant fishermen can buy worms in small earth-filled gunny bags sold by roadside vendors. Vundu, a tropical catfish, at 20kg (44lb) is Kariba's largest fish. It fancies ox heart and has been known to bite on blue washday soap. Spear fishing, too, is a popular sport among Kariba's angling enthusiasts.

Opposite: *Tourists explore the Zambezi by river boat.*
Above: *The lake is home to the handsome African fish eagle.* **Below:** *Fishing for the lake's plump bream.*

AFRICAN FISH EAGLE

Ten years ago it was believed that the use of the pesticide DDT in mosquito and tsetse fly control would wipe out the fish eagle on Lake Kariba. The bird has, however, proved tougher than the pundits. First recorded in southern Africa in 1800 at the Keurbooms River in the Cape, its echoing 'kow, kow' is one of the unforgettable sounds of Africa. The fish eagle is a common sight in the dead trees of Kariba's shore. Its nest is a huge untidy affair of sticks perched high in a tree.

Binga *

If you're a fisherman, then Binga, 200km (124 miles) northeast of Hwange, is worth considering. Binga, translated as 'thick woodland', is a small harbour and village originally built as an administrative centre for Tonga resettlement when the rising waters of Lake Kariba forced their evacuation 35 years ago.

The Tonga people have not really benefited from the translocation nor arguably from the school, hospital, supermarket and foreign-aid worker village. Their hunting skills are already dying as the wildlife in this western part of Kariba has long gone.

Binga has a few lakeside holiday homes, the new fully equipped **Chilila** and **Kulizwe** lodges and the attractive **Binga Rest Camp** with its hot-spring-fed pool. The village seems to provide employment for a good number of civil servants. The Kariangwe co-op 60km (37 miles) south of Binga is the best weekly buying spot for Tonga crafts. The crocodile farm in the village is not Jurassic Park, and Binga is not Sun City, but it is attracting increasing numbers of fisherfolk.

Kuburi
Wilderness Area **

The Zimbabwe Wildlife Society is fully aware of wildlife areas close to human habitation where animals or fauna could become threatened. One of these is the Kuburi Wilderness Area, bordering on the lake to the east of Kariba village, and now under the society's control. Originally part of the **Charara** and **Hurungwe hunting safari areas**, Kuburi reflects a variety of ecosystems ranging from

the open *Brachystegia* woodland of the Zambezi escarp-ment to mopane forests on the valley floor. It is broken, rough-hewn country looking onto the Kuburi hills, with the Zambezi gorge and the river downstream of Lake Kariba as its northern flank.

It has been divided into four areas, each with specific functions such as game-viewing drives, walking trails, educational tours, and camping. The area is quilted with a dozen rivers either flowing into Lake Kariba or the Zambezi. A game-viewing platform has been con-structed on the lake shore near the National Parks' **Nyanyana camp** and the Wildlife Society's campsite and headquarters. An ecological school has been built by the Lomagundi Hunters Association.

Although Kuburi has to contend with such enclaves as Kariba's airport, the main road to Harare and a banana farm (pay a visit to the crocodile farm), it is an area particularly exciting to young people. It has retained a tapestry of wildlife that ranges from lion and elephant to antbear and thicktailed bushbaby; there is also a galaxy of birds both at the water's edge and in the wood-lands, and the area is popular with anglers too.

Opposite: *Villagers process dried* kapenta, *a tiny sardine-like lake fish and a valuable source of protein.*
Above: *Trawling for* kapenta; *about 12,000 tonnes are netted in the lake each year.*

Lake Kariba at a Glance

June and **July** (winter) are the coolest, but even at higher altitudes such as Kariba Heights, the Zambezi valley is always hot (particularly October). Nights with a breeze are pleasant on a houseboat. December to February are rainy.

There are **daily flights** to Kariba from Victoria Falls, Hwange and Harare. The **tar road** from Harare is 365km (227 miles). If you decide to travel overland from Harare to Matusadona, a four-wheel-drive is advisable. There are light aircraft **airstrips** at Tashinga, Bumi, Fothergill, Chizarira, Tiger Bay, and Binga. Another option is the **car ferry** from Mlibizi to Kariba village. There is no rail, but **rural buses** are practically everywhere.

A **UTC bus** runs between airport and hotel resorts. **Taxis** available, as is **car hire**; call Europcar, tel: (161) 2321 (Cutty Sark Hotel); Avis, tel: (161) 2555; Hertz, tel: (161) 2662 (Lake View Inn). For backpackers, **rural buses** to Kariba and Binga from Harare. Kariba Ferries run **weekly cruises** to and from Mlibizi, tel: (161) 2460 or (14) 67661. On the lake, powerboats, yachts and houseboats can be hired. Transfers to safari-island lodges are via resort powerboats and small aircraft.

Lake Kariba
All hotels are perched on hills overlooking the lake.

Cutty Sark: possibly the most attractive rooms with a view, nice holiday restaurant, pub overlooks trees and lake, tel: (161) 2321.

Kariba Breezes: good marina when the lake is full, lovely dining room and thatched umbrellas by the pool, boat hire, tel: (161) 2433.

Lake View Inn: panoramic patio for candlelight dinners overlooking lake, very peaceful; craft shop, and crochet-work ladies in the car park, tel: (161) 2411.

Caribbea Bay: old Mexico architecture on lake shore, casino, large marina and water-skiing, call Zimbabwe Sun group, tel: (161) 2453.

Most High Hotel: bird's-eye view over the lake, family hotel, simple good value and friendly service (no liquor), tel: (161) 2964.

Tamarind Lodges: lovely self-catering cottages, recommended, tel: (161) 2697.

Camping and caravanning: Moth cottages and caravan park: tel: (161) 2809. Mopani Bay camping and caravan park: tel: (161) 2485. Caribbea Bay camping park: tel: (161) 2454.

West Kariba
Mlibizi Hotel: recently renovated chalets, horse riding, good fishing, gravel airstrip, tel: (115) 271 or (14) 67537.

Binga Resort: comfortable and attractive lake-shore chalets, tel: (115) 244.

Chilila Lodges: new, popular with fishermen, tel: (19) 72568.

Kulizwe Lodge, Binga: has a pool, tel: (115) 286.

Matusadona, Islands and Safari Lodges
Bumi Hills Safari Lodge: luxurious, perched on a cliff, elephant browse on the shoreline, tel: (161) 2353 or call Zimbabwe Sun group, tel: (14) 736644.

Sanyati Lodge: splendid isolation among trees on a rocky promontory for the reclusive few, tel: (14) 727881 or 738442.

Spurwing Island: informal, tents under thatch, small dining room, tel: (161) 2466.

Fothergill Island: largest of Matusadona's safari lodges, game-rich island surrounded by expanses of grass shore leading down to the lake, tel: (161) 2253, or (14) 707438 or 752974.

Tiger Bay: idyllic fisherman's haunt, three-sided chalets (fourth side is open, looking onto the Ume River), tel: (161) 2569.

Kuburi Wilderness: luxury tented camp; candles, crystal and silver dining beneath the stars, tel: (161) 2321.

Musango Safari Camp: luxury, tents under thatch, tel: (14) 796821.

Lake Kariba at a Glance

Charara Safari Lodges: nearest to Kariba town, double-storey thatch, tel: (14) 47129 or 750532.
Mswenzi Safari Lodge, Charara: three-bedroomed lodge on lake shore, tel: (168-5) 5955.
Chizarira Wilderness Safari Lodge: only lodge in Chizarira park; remote, quiet, wild and beautiful, tel: (113) 4637.
Ruzi Island: eight-bed lodge, reasonable rates, tel: (153) 2246.
Water Wilderness Safaris: personal wooden houseboats on Chiuri River, contact Zimbabwe Sun, tel: (161) 2353.
Katete Safari Lodge, near Bumi Hills: opening soon (Zimbabwe Sun), tel: (14) 736644.

National Parks Accommodation

All National Parks accommodation must be booked in Harare, tel: (14) 706077.
Chalets in 3 exclusive camps, maximum of 12 persons for minimum of 6 days on the Matusadona shore.
Camping at Nyanyana, 28km (17 miles) from Kariba; five camps on the Matusadona shore.
Bush camps: six exclusive camps, some with sleeping shelters, in Chizarira National Park.

WHERE TO EAT

The all-inclusive safari resorts have the best meals, served under the stars or open thatch. At all hotels in Kariba village, meals are usually served alfresco on verandahs and pool patios overlooking lake at night. Inexpensive meals available at the Country Club, tel: (161) 2283.

TOURS AND EXCURSIONS

Catalina Flying Boat: Nostalgia Safaris, tel: (14) 738999.
Catamaran sailing safaris: seven-yacht flotilla with mother ship; six passengers per yacht for six days, no sailing experience necessary, tel: (14) 335120, fax: 339483.
Crocodile farm: Lake Crocodile Park, 20km (12 miles) beyond airport, tel: (161) 2823.
Cruise Kariba: for full-day game-viewing to Matusadona islands, tel: (161) 2697.
Luxury lake cruises: Manica Travel Services, tel: (14) 703421; Lake Safaris, tel: (161) 2474; Kariba Breezes marina, tel: (161) 2433 or 2475; Kariba Yachts at Cutty Sark marina, tel: (161) 2983; Blue Water Charters, tel: (161) 2971.
Mississippi paddle steamer, MV Southern Belle: 32-man crew, 21 cabins, contact any travel agent, or try Phileas Fogg, tel: (14) 704141.

Photographic safaris: Chris Worden Safaris, tel: (161) 2321.
Tented safaris in Matusadona National Park: Muvimi Safaris, tel: (14) 793107.
Village tours: United Touring Company, tel: (161) 2321.
Walking safaris: in Chizarira, Backpackers Africa (subsidiary of Shearwater Adventures), tel: (113) 4471; also National Parks, tel: (14) 706077; walks in Matusadona, Safari Par Excellence, tel: (14) 750485.

USEFUL TELEPHONE NUMBERS

Boat maintenance and storage, Jays Engineering, tel: (161) 2538.
Houseboat hire, Africa Dawn Safaris, tel: (19) 46696; Zambezi Charters, tel: (161) 2336 or (14) 304474.
Kariba to Mlibizi Ferry, Kariba Ferries, for enquiries, tel: (14) 67661; to make reservations, tel: (161) 2460.
Kariba Publicity Association, tel: (161) 2328.
National Parks central booking office, tel: (14) 706077; Kariba branch, tel: (161) 2257; Matusadona branch, tel: (161) 2577.
Wildlife Society, Kuburi Wilderness, tel: (161) 2705.

KARIBA	J	F	M	A	M	J	J	A	S	O	N	D
AVERAGE TEMP. °F	78	78	78	76	71	65	65	71	80	85	83	79
AVERAGE TEMP. °C	26	26	26	21	21	19	19	22	27	29	29	26
Hours of Sun Daily	7	7	7	9	10	9	10	10	10	10	8	7
RAINFALL ins.	8	6	5	1.5	0	0	0	0	0	0.5	3	7
RAINFALL mm	196	160	121	35	5	0	1	0	1	16	80	189
Days of Rainfall	17	14	10	4	1	0	0	0	0	2	8	16

6
Zambezi Valley

For David Livingstone, the mighty **Zambezi** was God's highway to the interior, up which would flow the enlightened trade of England's scientific and industrial revolution bent on replacing the darkness of slavery. But the price he paid was dreadful; Livingstone's beloved wife, Mary, born in dry Kuruman on the other side of Africa, is buried on the river's watery banks. Livingstone's Zambezi journeys did end slavery, but a navigable river it was not to be; the **Cabora Bassa** rapids, site of today's dam, put paid to that.

Flanking the 300km stretch (186 miles) of the Zambezi from below Kariba Dam to the Mozambique border is the wildest and loveliest of Zimbabwe's wilderness areas. It has hippo in the muddy waters, crocodile on the river islands and beneath the shade of giant apple-ring acacia and mopane trees leading up to the escarpment, a wondrous profusion of wildlife and big game.

But its Garden of Eden fragility is continuously threatened by the possibility of uranium, coal and oil exploration and hydroelectric-power projects. It is also at risk from overgrazing by elephant, and its rhino have been decimated by poachers. The eradication of the tsetse fly may encourage the movement of cattle and man into the park, although cooperation between neighbouring small farmers, conservationists, safari hunters and ecotourism operators should obviate this problem.

There is no doubt, the lower Zambezi area, dominated by the **Mana Pools National Park**, offers superb opportunities for exhilarating close encounters in the wild.

CLIMATE

The valley can be hellishly **hot**, and **humid** as Rangoon, but this changes in winter with a breeze off the river and mists above the water. September is a good month: the migrant birds arrive and wildlife concentrates at the river; June and July are the most comfortable. At 400m (1312ft), the valley temperature never drops much below 20°C (68°F). The **rainy Christmas season** makes the flood plains impossible to cross, even for big trucks.

Opposite: *Guests of an exclusive lodge at Mana Pools view game at leisure.*

DON'T MISS

*** A canoeing safari on the Zambezi
*** National Parks' 3- to 6-day walking trails
*** Late-afternoon game-viewing at Long Pool
** Bream or tigerfishing on the Zambezi
** Bird-watching (keep a checklist); try identifying trees, too.
** Three nights in a riverside safari lodge
* A meal at Cloud's End in Makuti (meet the locals).

MANA POOLS NATIONAL PARK

Heart of the middle Zambezi valley, this beautiful national park stretches inland from the river, through twisting apple-ring acacia and 100-year-old mahogany trees to the baobabs and mopane scrub of the great escarpment, and then along the river for 50km (31 miles). It is surrounded by the **Hurungwe**, **Sapi**, **Chewore** and **Dande** hunting areas. Mana Pools is one of the few wildlife areas where one can walk freely, and the richness and variety of its animals is renowned.

The nearest human habitation is at **Kanyemba**, where canoeing safaris end, on the border with Mozambique. The headwaters of the huge Cabora Bassa Dam – as large as Lake Kariba – lie off Kanyemba. Across the river and close to the shore are the high mountains of the Zambian escarpment, unfortunately not a World Heritage Site like Mana Pools. The park is open from May to the end of October; National Parks has lodges at Nyamepi, as well as camping sites spread out along the river.

The southern edge of where the Zambezi used to flow many thousands of years ago is marked by a change of vegetation from mopane woodland and fussy jesse bush to riverine trees. Here, the terraces are rich in alluvial soils. A little way inland from the river and to the west of the camp is Long Pool, one of several pools that give Mana its name. It holds water year-round and in the hot, dry months is a magnet to animals. The river banks support an abundance of birdlife, and the pools are frequented by hippo and crocodile; Mana is known, too, for its clawless otter and honey badger.

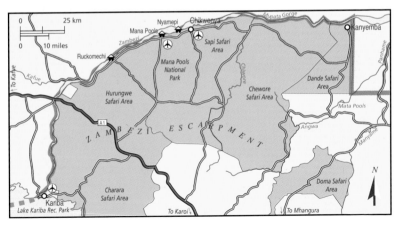

The Flood Plains ★★★

Contrary to the name 'flood plains', the rains before and after Christmas fill Mana's pans and pools rather than the swollen Zambezi. No doubt there were occasional raging floods in years gone by, but today, with the river flow controlled at Lake Kariba, that is unlikely. The Zambezi has, however, caused river-bank erosion. At Mana the river is wide, with islands, sandbanks and high escarpments to either side.

On the fertile terraces, as the Mana plains are called, grow huge forests of apple-ring thorn-trees (*Acacia albida*), much loved by high-reaching elephant, and the smaller woolly podded and blue-thorn varieties. There are also the monkey-thorn trees and Natal mahogany (whose bark is soaked in water and used in traditional medicine as an emetic; hence its Latin name *Trichilia emetica*). Tamarind, fig, sausage and rain trees add to the biodiversity. And then there are the waterbuck, elephant, buffalo, nyala, jackal, hippo and a constant chorus of up to 350 species of birds. Drifting past the banks in a canoe is an unforgettable way to go game-viewing.

In the dry season the flood plains are brown and dessicated, the trees thin-leaved and thirsty, with the grass cover and the lower branches of the trees stripped bare by grazing animals, many of whom die if the rains do not come. Then in November the heavens open, and soon the park is a lush jungle with huge pools, flowering trees, marshes with pink morning glory and a deep umbrella of huge green trees: paradise revisited. Soon, however, the animals leave the river to trek inland to quieter, select, and now well-watered territories.

Above: *A village woman of the Zambezi River valley grinds cassava.*

THE HONEY BADGER

The honey badger is one of the world's fiercest and most aggressive animals; it will always stand its ground and has been known, if annoyed, to take on lion. Nocturnal, often solitary, it is jet-black in colour with a white nose-to-tail saddle and it walks like a drunken sailor. The badger sniffs around for baboon spiders, scorpions and, of course, honey. If it smells food at a safari camp, it will claw and bite its way through a wooden door.

Ruckomechi **

Ruckomechi River has its headwaters on the plateau not far from the town of Karoi. It flows down the escarpment and joins the Zambezi 40km (25 miles) east of Zimbabwe's northern border post of Chirundu, overlooking the mountains of the Zambian escarpment across a wide stretch of the Zambezi. A particularly lush band of acacia and mahogany stretches right to the edge of the high river bank, with the fast-swirling river below. In the shade of these trees is the luxury **Ruckomechi Camp**, voted the best safari lodge in Zimbabwe, and catering for a maximum of 20 people. On the island in the river clusters of hippo and lazy lines of crocodile congregate (one recent Christmas morning, a group of visitors was observed playing cricket there!).

Elephant and buffalo wander past the thatched chalets and usually in the evening to the bar–lounge, which offers a viewpoint over the river. Activities arranged at the camp include game-viewing by canoe or as part of guided wilderness walks. There is, incongruously, a small conference centre at Ruckomechi, and more appropriately, children's bush-orientation courses during the off-season summer months. The camp operates from April to November, with access from Chirundu usually via powerboat. Otherwise, Chikwenya has an airport, with road access between the camps.

Above: *The sinister-looking Nile crocodile, found in great numbers along the lower reaches of the Zambezi River.*

Ecotourism in the Zambezi Valley **

Much of Zimbabwe's wildlife heritage and 75% of the middle Zambezi area near Mana Pools is set aside for high-income-generating hunting. There are nearly 40 big-game hunters in Zimbabwe, with more concentrating on plains game – mainly antelope – while others have mixed-game and cattle ranches. Bird shoots and bow hunting are also favoured.

Sport hunting to many is anathema. Others maintain that its profitability preserves the wildlife. A recent compromise has been the camp-fire ecotourism concept whereby small farmers living in communal lands adjacent to game areas benefit directly from fees paid by hunters; as do district councils anxious to build a clinic or school. This highly successful profit-sharing exercise has encouraged subsistence farmers to preserve the wildlife and its habitats.

Hopefully one day, with a sustainable balance reached between man and nature, it will do away with the need to have exclusive wildlife parks or reserves. Perhaps too man will, like the peoples of Namibia, take sufficient pride in the animals to eliminate the need for fences and regulations – as well as guns.

HORSES OF THE ZAMBEZI

Hippo is Greek for 'water horse', of which there are some 3000 along this stretch of the Zambezi. Flotillas of hippo are known as pods. A hippo can submerge and walk along the bottom for up to 10 minutes, but still hear, smell and see as if it were on the surface. It weighs up to 2 tonnes, can outrun a man, and easily destroys a boat. Hippo are possibly responsible for more human fatalities than any other animal (yawning is a territorial display or sign of aggression).

A hippo's weak spot is the skin on its back; trapped out of water for any length of time, the sun will crack and lacerate it.

Left: *The pristine splendour of Mana Pools; its riverine terraces, seasonal pools and channels are a magnet for huge numbers of big game.*

Right: *Canoeists explore the lower Zambezi along the Mana Pools section. The wildlife is at its most prolific during the dry season, when the game comes down from the escarpment to graze on the lush flood plain.* **Opposite:** *Egrets hitch a buffalo ride. The lower Zambezi is home to around 16,000 of these large mammals, which are, interestingly, relatives of the antelope.*

VALLEY PEOPLE

Where Zambia's Kafue River joins the Zambezi lies the excavated **Ingombe Ilede** burial ground of seven exceptionally wealthy **Mbara** ruler–traders. The tomb was rich in copper crosses (the universal money of Africa 500 years ago), wire, hoes and iron gongs (symbol of kings and originally invented in West Africa). Mbara funeral clothes were cotton wraps from India while their jewellery included shell necklaces coated in gold. Their pottery is possibly the finest of ancient Zimbabwe. The Mbara travelled far and wide, trading first with the Arabs, then the Portuguese.

Canoeing Safaris ★★★

Like the water people of the Okavango Delta in neighbouring Botswana, and the Sena of the Zambezi Delta, the Tonga, Kalolo and Korekore fishermen (among others), have long used dugout canoes to navigate and fish on the Zambezi. In recent years, the habit has caught on among river adventurers, this time in fibreglass two-man Canadian canoes, usually in groups of two or three and led by an experienced river guide. Tourists are not expected to be accomplished canoeists, and they can usually learn much from their guide in terms of fauna and flora. Canoeing safaris have become the fashionable way to do Africa. There are several companies now offering canoe trips down the Zambezi, ranging in length from three to nine days. Strictly controlled, only one party daily is permitted per stretch of river.

The Zambezi is largely an easy-going river (although the **Mupata gorge** whirlpools, an optional section, add adrenaline) and the silence and gentle progress of the canoes facilitates close-to-shore game-viewing. From sandbank to sandbank, hippo act as stop streets, crocodile divert, buffalo stare balefully, and a myriad waders

constantly tiptoe in the shallows. You camp at night, often on a sandbank, with chilled wine, good food and philosophy beneath the stars. Near Mupata gorge, the towering red cliffs seem to glow after sundown. Mosquito nets are suspended from paddles stuck in the sand and act as deterrents to predators. Stay awake if you like (there may be hyena to listen out for). They won't bother you, unless you show a leg outside your net … Or you can listen to the snorting hippo.

Canoe trips can start in the narrow gorge below Kariba's dam wall and go as far as **Chirundu**; or you can add another three days to go as far as **Mana Pools**, and a further three to **Kanyemba** where Zambia, Zimbabwe and Mozambique all meet.

One has to learn to 'read' the water, almost like tracking. Near **Chikwenya** there are so many 'river horses' that safari guides nickname it 'hippo city'. Trolling for tigerfish or watching the carmine bee-eaters, one covers about 20km (12 miles) a day. The best time to paddle is early morning, resting in the heat of the day. A gusty wind can sometimes blow up suddenly on the river.

FUN IN THE SUN

Africa is synonymous with sunshine. And every day in Zimbabwe, there are usually sunny skies. However, sunburn can lead to skin cancer, particularly on the ears, nose and forehead. Use a factor 15 sun cream and wear a hat, preferably with a wide brim. Sun reflected off grass is half as powerful as full overhead sunlight and off water can be very damaging.

Chikwenya ★★

At Chikwenya on the eastern edge of Mana Pools National Park, Zambia's hills – particularly at sunset – seem far away across the Zambezi. This is, in fact, the widest stretch of the middle Zambezi as it forks to either side of **Chikwenya Island**; here the Sapi, a seasonal, usually sandy river joins it. A series of floods in the 1930s cut the island off from the high forested river bank. It was named many years ago after Chief Chikwenya and means 'a scratchy place', whether referring to the need for elephants to scratch their backs or lions their claws is uncertain.

There is an airstrip at Chikwenya; canoes and a boat are available for river drifting.

On the edge of the Sapi River and set back a little from the Zambezi is **Chikwenya Safari Camp**. It is wilder and smaller than Ruckomechi and is ideal for walking trails, particularly up the dry riverbed with its huge riverine trees, troops of trek baboon and browsing elephant. It is normal to take an armed guide, although on their own these men of the valley are usually only armed with a thumbed *Roberts'* bird book.

Above: *A Tonga woman enjoys her 'bubble pipe', fashioned from a calabash, or gourd. The Tonga, relocated further inland when the dam at Kariba was built, do not lead an easy existence; originally fisherpeople, they survive these days from farming on the arid soils along the perimeter of Matusadona National Park.*

Guests dine beneath a canopy of huge trees overlooking distant plains and the river, and observe the passing animal cavalcade from a wonderful hide–platform.

At night by paraffin lamp it is animal anecdote time: who encountered this, who encountered that (in fact, mosquito nets are used in safari camps only partly for mosquitoes; they also deflect other curious visitors). Behind the camp impala fidget. There may even be a leopard about, keen to deposit a partially gnawed ram in one of Chikwenya Camp's choice of trees.

Zambezi Valley at a Glance

BEST TIMES TO VISIT

September (spring) is probably the best month. The **coolest** months are **June** and **July**. Mana Pools National Park is closed November to end April, but canoeing safaris occur year-round except for mid-January to end February.

GETTING THERE

Light aircraft takes you into Chikwenya. Overland to Mana Pools National Park a four-wheel-drive is needed to go via the parks office at Marongora, 24km (15 miles) north of Makuti on the Great North road to Zambia. You also need a four-wheel-drive from Chirundu, flanking the river, to Ruckomechi Safari Lodge (usually done by powerboat).

GETTING AROUND

Access is limited, hitchhiking is not allowed and one has to register with National Parks either at Harare or Marongora. Much of the region is safari hunting area. **Walking** is permitted in the national park at one's own risk. **Game drives** are plentiful. No powered craft are allowed; **canoes** and other craft can only be launched at designated spots. Boating in Zambian waters could result in your craft being impounded (the border runs centre of the main channel). For **air charter** services, contact Executive Air, tel: (14) 302184; United Air, tel: (14) 731713; or Safari Transfers, tel: (14) 302422.

WHERE TO STAY

Ruckomechi Safari Lodge: contact Shearwater Adventures, tel: (14) 735712.
Chikwenya Safari Camp: call Fothergill Island Safaris, tel: (14) 707438 or 752974.
Kayila Lodge near Mana Pools: river-bank luxury, Safari Par Excellence, tel: (14) 720527.
Chalets and camping sites: prebook with National Parks (there is a choice of four campsites, named after fish), tel: (14) 706077.

Accommodation en route
Cloud's End Hotel or **Bwana Game Hilltop Hunting Motel**, Makuti: hot, hilly, rugged terrain, hunting trophies adorn pub walls, tel: (163) 526.
Albida Safari Lodge, Chirundu: tree-house accommodation for six people, overlooking Zambezi River, tel: (14) 795686.
Mavuradonha Wilderness Camp: self-catering A-frame huts and rondavels, bring everything, call the Wildlife Society, tel: (14) 731596.

WHERE TO EAT

Luxury safari lodges provide all meals and drinks, as do canoeing and other safaris; apart from these, there are no restaurants. Bring all your own food and equipment. Makuti is the last place for (limited) stores and petrol before entering Mana Pools National Park.

TOURS AND EXCURSIONS

Canoeing safaris: Shearwater Adventures offer the widest range, tel: (14) 735712, or try: Bushlife Zimbabwe, tel: (14) 48548; Gwembe Trails, tel: (14) 729621; Safari Par Excellence, tel: (14) 750485; Zambezi Trails, tel: (14) 705040.
Game-viewing foot safaris (at Mana Pools): you're on your own; check in at the ranger's office first if you can. **Guided safaris** (four to six days) offered by Ruckomechi Safari Lodge through Backpackers Africa, tel: (14) 735712; also National Parks.

USEFUL TELEPHONE NUMBERS

National Parks central booking office, tel: (14) 706077.
National Parks (Marongora), tel: (163) 533.
Zimbabwe Association of Tour and Safari Operators, and **Zimbabwe Professional Hunters and Guides Association**, tel: (14) 733211, fax: 723230.

ZAMBEZI VALLEY	J	F	M	A	M	J	J	A	S	O	N	D
AVERAGE TEMP. °F	78	78	78	76	71	65	65	71	80	85	83	79
AVERAGE TEMP. °C	26	26	26	21	21	19	19	22	27	29	29	26
Hours of Sun Daily	7	7	7	9	10	9	10	10	10	10	8	7
RAINFALL ins.	8	6	5	1.5	0	0	0	0	0	0.5	3	7
RAINFALL mm	196	160	121	35	5	0	1	0	1	16	80	189
Days of Rainfall	17	14	10	4	1	0	0	0	0	2	8	16

7
Eastern Highlands

The massifs, downs and mountain forests of the Eastern Highlands stretch for 300km (186 miles), dividing the highveld of Zimbabwe from the tropical lowlands of Mozambique. **Mutare** is the area capital, accessed by road and rail from Harare in the west and Mozambique's Beira port on the Indian Ocean.

The Highlands comprise three mountain groups: **Nyanga** (the largest and most popular), **Bvumba** and **Chimanimani**. Nyanga is typical of the area, cooler than the Bvumba, which, with its silent 'b', conjures up the sound of rivers in mountain chasms and thunder in the hills; the latter also experiences a higher rainfall. Chimanimani, sited on the massif crest, is windswept and at times can be exceptionally cold. It is, however, a hiker's paradise, offering many enjoyable and often challenging walks (if the holiday you plan is a walking one, it's worth contacting the Mountain Club of Zimbabwe). Chimanimani is smaller than Nyanga, but it is wilder.

All sparsely populated, these highland areas are geared for lonely-as-a-cloud hiking, archaeological snooping, horse riding, golfing, trout fishing and eagle spotting. The area is a bird-watcher's treasure trove.

It is not African big-game country but the mountains, with their fragrant heather-and-fern winds, have always been for the farmers and city dwellers a respite from drought and stress. Although the log fires are essential for the freezing winter nights, they also burn during the day, setting the perfect scene for cosy get-togethers and wholesome, soul-warming cream teas.

CLIMATE

In the Highlands the air is **much cooler** than anywhere else in Zimbabwe, often **very cold** in **June** and **July**, and the mountain and forest surrounds encourage the year-round burning of log fires in the hotels. **Rains** fall from **November** through **March**, when many of the wildflowers bloom. In spring (August), the new, young leaves on the msasa trees set the mountain slopes afire with a quilt of auburn, brown, red and gold.

Opposite: *Emerald-green tea estates grace many of the Eastern Highlands' slopes and valleys.*

DON'T MISS

*** A picnic-lunch excursion to the Nyahokwe Mountain ruins and Ziwa Field Museum
*** A round of golf in intoxicating mountain scenery
*** A drive through the misty Bvumba mountains, stopping for tea in the Botanical Gardens
*** A bracing day's hiking in the Chimanimani mountains
** A scenic drive to Pungwe gorge and Mutarazi Falls
** Skyline Drive between Chimanimani and Chipinge (bridge built by Italian PoWs, Moodie's Grave, Chirinda Forest); take lunch.

Opposite: *A challenging golf course in the highlands.*

NYANGA
Nyanga National Park ***

Nyanga, in the northernmost part of the Eastern Highlands, with its forests, waterfalls, rivers, open moorland and solitude, is larger than England's Dartmoor but not dissimilar. Its grassy mountain slopes and downs were once covered with woodlands and supported Iron Age agricultural populations who depleted the tree cover and left a legacy of tumbled stone terracing. The southern sector of the park is the wildest.

Lakes **Udu**, **Rhodes** and **Nyangwe** (also known as Mare) are surrounded by evergreen forest, reeds, lilies, sweeps of mountain terrain, and National Parks cottages. A trout hatchery supplies anglers, and pony trails afford a fine opportunity to appreciate the beautiful scenery.

Mount Nyangani, Zimbabwe's highest at 2593m (8508ft), is a favoured climb. Nyanga is not a game park but there are kudu, wildebeest, waterbuck, leopard, side-striped jackal and reedbuck; it is also rich in birdlife.

The **Pungwe gorge**, **Mutarazi Falls**, Nyangombe River and the villages of Nyanga and Juliasdale are easily accessible by gravel road. The area once belonged to Cecil John Rhodes, and his homestead is now a hotel and museum.

The Eastern Highlands embrace numerous private nature sanctuaries and game reserves; the right approach coupled with a genuine interest in birds, botany or beauty will usually assure entry.

Nyanga's Ancient Ruins ★★

There are hundreds of hill-top, stone-walled enclosures and lichen-grey ruins in Nyanga National Park: walls constructed of hand-cut blocks, corrals, stock pits, terraced fields and *kopje* forts. The agricultural terraces were made in an effort to clear the stony ground and retain the soil in a mountainous region of heavy rains.

Make a point of visiting the ancient hill-top structures of **Nyahokwe** and the new field museum to the side of **Ziwa Mountain**, valley sentinel to the west of Nyanga. Look out for the tiny crossroads **sculpture park**. An informative National Museums guide will show you the old iron-smelting furnace, then take you up the winding mountain track past flame lilies and the four *musha*, or homes of lesser chiefs, to the massive stone-built corral of the chief with its *dare* (meeting venue). On the saddle of Nyahokwe, the views of Nyanga's mountains are panoramic. **Ziwa Museum**, surrounded by the stone structures of what must have been a large community, presents a superb picture of the lifestyle of the Nyanga iron-smelting craftsmen, builders and farmers of 300 years ago. There are picnic shelters nearby.

Nyangani ★★★

In Nyanga, one's eyes are continuously diverted to the mountain, Nyangani, which can be seen from anywhere in the park, and from as far away as 100km (60 miles). The mountain club has marked out a two-hour hike up to Nyangani's peak.

A great swathe on the skyline, the mountain is frequently topped with a duvet of cloud as it descends in folds of undulating bare hills to the rivers and lakes it has fostered. From the lush Honde, it rises a sheer 1200m (3937ft) from the valley floor.

MOUNTAIN TRAILS

- Nyazengu: full-day, 12km (7.5 miles); entrance fee
- Nyangani: straight up Zimbabwe's highest mountain, 4 hours
- Nyangombe Falls: past Udu Mountain and lodges, 5km (3 miles)
- Nyamaziwa River: picnic trip to pool and cascades, 1.5km (1 mile)
- Nyangani to Pungwe drift: full-day, broken gravel road, 22km (13.5 miles)
- Udu Dam: circular, over or around Udu Hill, 1–3 hours
- Temburatedza Falls to Pungwe Pools: steep drop, 5km (3 miles).

Above: *Angling for trout along the scenically stunning reaches of the Pungwe River.*

Nyazengu Nature Reserve ★★★

Tucked against Nyangani's flank and surrounded by the national park is the privately owned 1250ha (3089 acres) Nyazengu Nature Reserve. On a winter's morning, wisps of mist alternate with sunlight on the high massif, making the 12km (7.5 miles) trail drop-dead gorgeous. In summer it offers a cornucopia of proteas and minute flowers; black eagles ride the thermals above the salmon-trout pools near the owner's cottage, 5km (3 miles) from Nyangani car park.

The trail wanders in and out of montane forest, then grasslands, dropping steeply to the Nyazengu River and waterfall. Passing through another forest, it emerges onto a plateau, the slag from ancient iron workings at your feet; the trail then takes you on a fairyland downhill walk of tangled forest, falls, pools and streams.

Be prepared for sudden storms, mist and intense cold. Nyazengu's rich and varied wildlife has been known to include leopard and lion, while in the river forest near the falls, it is possible to glimpse the emerald-ruby flight of a Livingstone's loerie.

Pungwe Gorge ★★

Pungwe gorge, a 10km (6 miles) forested cleft in the Nyanga escarpment, leads down to the **Honde Valley**. At the view site, the Pungwe (largest of Nyanga's 17 rivers) rushes over the lip of the escarpment in an explosion of roaring water. One can drive across the Pungwe drift, astride which sit two remote National Parks bungalows; the approach road passes through pine and wattle plantations, and fruit farms. The gorge, reputed to be an old gold-traders' route, is rich in montane hardwoods,

---

TROUT FISHING

Nyanga's dams and rivers offer the best trout fishing in the Highlands. An average-size catch weighs 1kg (2.2 lb), the record, 3.8kg (8.4 lb). The best rivers are the Nyangombe and the Nyamaziwa, while Gulliver and Purdon are the quality dams. In 1931, fingerlings introduced into the Odzani produced the first catch. There is a hatchery at Nyangwe Dam (Mare) and a trout-farming industry in the mountains, as well as a considerable number of privately owned dams and streams for fishing.

ferns, overhead orchids and the occasional gaboon viper (*see* panel). The **Temburatedza Falls** and the crystal pools of the **Matendere River** can be visited nearby.

Mutarazi National Park **

Forming the southernmost slice of the Nyanga park is the Mutarazi National Park. Its two features are the view of the Honde and the 762m (2500ft) **Mutarazi Falls**, second highest in Africa. A wildflower-strewn path hugs the mountain down to the promontory view site, which seems to hang suspended over the Honde valley. Behind, the slender spume of the falls floats endlessly downwards to the rain forest. A National Parks campsite with basic facilities is situated above the falls, near the car park and picnic tables.

Locked in by the Nyanga massif and the mountains of Mozambique, the hot, humid Honde valley produces tropical fruits, and at **Aberfoyle**, export quality tea. The 100m-high (328ft) masimike granite needles jutting up from the valley floor provide an interesting feature. Each day hardy residents climb 10km (6 miles) up from the Honde valley to their workplaces on the escarpment.

Troutbeck **

By Troutbeck, locals mean not the tiny village but **Troutbeck Inn**, with its lake, golf course, wooded hills and foyer log fire that's never extinguished. Above the resort are the **Connemara lakes** and the National Trust's **World's View** overlooking, it seems, the whole of Zimbabwe. Higher still is a ruined fort complex.

The Nyamaropa road east of Troutbeck leads past seed-potato and tulip

> ### EXCITING BITING
>
> The gaboon viper is Zimbabwe's star snake. Its coat of many colours – yellow, brown and purple triangles – added to its length, weight, huge head and fangs, and above all, its deadly bite, send shivers through one's imagination. It lives deep in dark mountain forests (but rarely in the Bvumba). One Zimbabwean family keeps several as pets!

The chacma baboon lives in mountains and riverine woodland, surviving on wild fruit, roots and bulbs. Here a baboon makes a meal of water lilies.

farms, then drops 1500m (4922ft) in 15 minutes to the Mozambique border and runs into Nyanga North, a partially tar, circular route ending in Nyanga village, with its vegetable market, craft village, rug-weaving co-op, library, church and Village Inn. New roads are currently being constructed in Nyanga that will not only connect areas such as the remote **Gleneagles** on the eastern slopes of the mountains (Zimbabwe's highest rainfall area) with the Aberfoyle tea plantations, but also the rugged baobab country of Nyanga North.

BVUMBA
Mutare *

High palms march down the centre of Herbert Chitepo, Mutare's main street in this, Zimbabwe's fifth-largest town, which has a population of 100,000. It sits in the lee of the Bvumba in a valley encircled by mountains. Named after a local river meaning 'piece of metal' (probably gold) Mutare lies in the mountain gap through which Zimbabwe's road and rail links pass to Mozambique. The road from Harare and Nyanga to this fruit, rail, timber and tourist town comes winding down over **Christmas Pass**, and at night the town is a bowl of lights far below. Mutare was originally sited further north, but was relocated with the arrival of the railway from Beira. Old Mutare now has the **Methodist Africa University**.

There is a good museum, a nature reserve at **Cecil Kop** run by the Wildlife Society, an aloe garden with 10,000 specimens, and the unusual Roman Catholic cathedral. **Sakubva market** is fun, **Murahwa's Hill** has Iron Age ruins, Mutare Heights road offers the best view of the town, while philanthropist–poet Kingsley Fairbridge's house, Utopia, portrays colonial living.

LEOPARD ROCK

The Leopard Rock Hotel is framed and shaded by ancient gnarled trees, their roots twisting around boulders. Behind the pink chateau's turrets, the mountain of Chinyakwaremba (meaning 'hill of tired legs') stands sentinel. From the hotel's umbrella-shaded patio, the view is of rolling emerald gardens, the golf course, and range beyond range of blue-green mist-covered mountains. A more idyllic setting would be difficult to visualize. The hotel itself and the individual rooms are Camelot-sumptuous. The entrance foyer of black marble and white Grecian columns has a two-storey-high glass panel with a planetarium view onto a botanical wonderland. The overall feel is luxury liner of yesteryear rather than a modern resort.

There are two roads from Nyanga down to Mutare, one via Penhalonga, an old gold-mining frontier town 17km (11 miles) from Mutare. At the southern exit is the **Pioneer Sisters Memorial**, one-time hospital site for three nursing sisters who, 100 years ago, walked 241km (150 miles) from Beira to nurse the prospectors. The plaques, the iron gate dating back to 1853, flowers, mountains and trees make it a pretty picnic spot. **La Rochelle's** tiered gardens nearby is another alternative.

Bvumba Botanical Gardens ***

Bvumba, with its own miniclimate, is a forested, mountainous, and often mist-cocooned promontory jutting into Mozambique. It is favoured by protea farmers, retired couples and, increasingly, holiday-makers (particularly birders, for here the rare Roberts' prinia, among others, can be found). The road to the Bvumba starts in Mutare's industrial sites and ends among coffee farms past the elegant pink turreted Leopard Rock Hotel.

The Bvumba Botanical Gardens and Reserve include a 30ha (74 acres) English country garden of azaleas, fuchsias, hydrangeas, lilies, and annuals set amidst pathways, wooden bridges, streams and lakes. There is also a tea shoppe. Many more hectares of indigenous preserved woodland overlook the casual splendour of Lake Chicamba Real in Mozambique, 1000m (3280ft) below.

The indigenous rain forest of the **Bunga Botanical Reserve** straddles the main road just before the gardens. Its well-laid-out paths are for the serious student of trees, ferns, butterflies and wildflowers. Given to the nation by Sir Lionel

Opposite: *Panorama of Mutare, attractive capital of the eastern region.*
Below: *The enchanting Bridal Veil waterfall.*

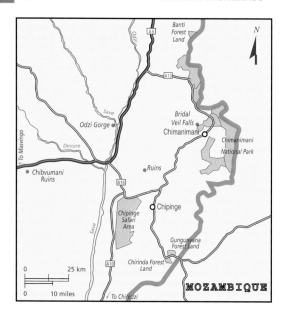

Cripps, its entrance is marked by three plaques and a lovely roadside picnic site.

Burma Valley ★
Big farm plantations of coffee, banana and pineapple, combined with the Zimunya communal lands of maize, cotton and tobacco, occupy either end of the loop road into the Essex and Burma valleys lying beneath the Bvumba Heights. The two valleys are laced with rivers and face the Mozambique hills.

COFFEE – WITH CREAM?

Originally native to Arabia (those thimble cupfuls in the desert), coffee growing began in Zimbabwe in 1900, in the Chimanimani area, joined 50 years later by the Bvumba; some of Zimbabwe's best coffee is now grown on the Bvumba's lower slopes. The Arabica berries are picked off the bushes, soaked to free the kernels, then roasted. Much is exported, although world prices do greatly fluctuate. There are superb dams, forests, scenically exciting horse rides and walks on the coffee farms, particularly below and around Leopard Rock; all it takes is to find a friendly farmer.

CHIMANIMANI NATIONAL PARK

When viewed from tiny Chimanimani village's Raj-like hotel 10km (6 miles) away, the national park is a great granite wall, smouldering blue and impregnable in the early morning. Its highest peaks, **Kweza** (Binga), **Mawenje** and **Dombe**, exceed 2200m (7218ft).

Accessible only by foot and crisscrossed with paths, lakes, caves, streams, gorges and stone forests, it is a hiker's paradise of undisturbed fauna and flora. The park covers an area half the size of Nyanga but is much wilder. Geologists believe the Chimanimani, part of the African Frontier System, came into existence millions of years ago when the area's white quartzite massif crunched and cracked into folds against the plateau.

Two-thirds of the Chimanimani range is in Mozambique; the park is seldom more than 7km (4 miles) wide and it is easy to stray into Zimbabwe's neighbour. This is fine for locals, but after a 15-year guerrilla war in which land mines played a major part, one should be sensible; and the border is certainly not marked with orange-and-white cones. So keep to the known routes.

Tessa's Pool (named after a Harare schoolteacher) and rope swing on the Hadange River will refresh you en route to the ranger-manned **Mutekeswane Base Camp**, 19km (12 miles) from Chimanimani village, and the usual entry point to the mountains. There are in fact three routes up, ascending a height of 500m (1641ft) which takes about three hours to do. The usual one is Bailey's Folly, to the mountain hut.

Walking in the Chimanimani is serious stuff – it is straight up and over the first peaks, so prepare accordingly: make sure you have good hiking shoes, a litre of water, hat, food, perhaps a compass. All the water along the way is drinkable; caves provide shelter. Keep an eye out for snakes and sudden storms.

There are good walks from the stone mountain-hut: 40 minutes to **Skeleton Pass** is one. Others include the all-day Banana Grove trail to the **Southern Lakes**, and a three-hour climb up **Mount Binga** (2437m; 7996ft), among many others. A good place to camp is **Digby's Cave** which has a waterfall and pool. Further on is **Peterhouse Cave**, named after a Zimbabwean school.

The **Bundi plateau** with its cracked strata formations, proteas and grassy vistas is, some say, like Table Mountain but more so. It's also very wild.

BRIDAL VEIL FALLS

West of Chimanimani village is the perfect picnic spot: a grassy bank facing the high lacery of the Bridal Veil Falls, with its banana-like tree ferns, lianas, moss-covered rocks, clear pool and lush vegetation. The thin tributary of the Nyahodi River cascades softly down a series of 25 green steps. In the surrounding msasa valleys – a two-hour walk from Chimanimani – the birdlife is rich.

Left: *The rugged terrain of the Nyanga and Chimanimani mountain ranges, in particular, offers hikers stimulating walks enhanced by magnificent sweeping vistas.*

Chimanimani also has some of the world's deepest caves. One of them, **Jungle Pot**, goes down 250m (820ft) and is the sixth deepest of its type in the world.

At the southern end of Chimanimani National Park, deep in the valley and almost on the Mozambique border, are the two **Haroni Rusitu** botanical forest reserves. Schoolchildren in the area are helping the Chipinge Wildlife Society protect these rain forests and their ecologically threatened and rare birdlife, their trees, and animals such as the tree civet. For the serious bird-watcher, the forests harbour such specimens as the chestnut-fronted helmet shrike and red-winged warbler.

An **Outward Bound School**, part of the worldwide organization, is at the base of the Chimanimani massif.

Hot Springs *

In the low-lying, bee-farming communal area flanking the **Odzi River** 86km (53 miles) from Mutare are the hot springs near **Nyanyadzi**. These mineral springs have been turned into a resort, something of an oasis in the surrounding bare lowveld. Rich in sodium sulphate and bicarbonate, the waters are believed to be good for ailments such as rheumatism and arthritis. Thatched en-suite lodges using generated electricity surround a central lake. The birdlife is particularly prolific.

Below: *A charming thatched lodge overlooks the river at Hot Springs.* **Opposite:** *Birchenough Bridge, gateway to the Chimanimani mountains.*

One of Zimbabwe's first irrigation schemes was started in 1919 at Nyanyadzi by a Mount Selinda missionary. Today communal farms produce good grain and fruit crops, particularly mangoes.

Also in the lowveld is **Birchenough Bridge**. In 1984, 49 years after its construction, this 330m (1083ft) steel-arch bridge – looking like a silver half-moon across the sandy

Save River – had its bridge deck widened and strengthened by the same British company who designed and built the original one. Named after the chairman of the British South Africa Company, the superstructure contains 1540 tonnes of high-tensile steel; during construction, technology and equipment from Sydney Harbour's bridge were utilized. The Birchenough Bridge links Beira port, Mutare, Chipinge and Chimanimani with Masvingo and South Africa.

Chirinda Forest Botanical Reserve **

Chipinge is a small, high-rainfall farming town of 10,000 people with an air of 'Let's settle this at twenty paces'. It has coffee, tea, pine and wattle plantations, a hotel that serves good breakfasts and a club that welcomes visitors. Dating back to what is known as the Moodie Trek (Thomas Moodie was a Scottish Afrikaner), you will still hear Afrikaans spoken here.

South of Chipinge is the Chirinda Forest Botanical Reserve, which surrounds the American-founded mission station of **Mount Selinda**. Chirinda is a tropical hardwood forest of some 100 tree species, and the last remaining tract of primeval forest in the country. When exploring, start with the **Big Tree** or **Valley of the Giants** tracks. The Big Tree, now probably dying, is a 1000-year-old red mahogany, nearly 60m (197ft) high and 16m (52ft) round. There are many other trees, including the unique zebra wood, ironwoods, figs, mosses, ferns, orchids, parasite creepers – and butterflies.

A rather weather-beaten **Swynnerton's Memorial** near the mission records the work of the British naturalist who came to Chimanimani in 1898. What is known today about the reserve's unique flora and fauna is largely due to Swynnerton's invaluable recordings.

WILDFLOWERS THAT DELIGHT

The first Westerner to comment on Zimbabwe's 5000 flowering plants and ferns was Portuguese Dominican friar, Iaoa Dos Santos, in 1609. The subject close to his heart was the dead-but-now-alive resurrection plant (when dry it forms a tight ball, but once moistened it unfolds and blooms). Africa's wildflowers are usually small, often only tiny flashes of blue, red or yellow at one's feet. The blue pentanisia and pink Manica daisy are only two; the glorious red-and-yellow flame lily graces the wilderness after the rains. Picking them is tempting but eco-hostile.

Eastern Highlands at a Glance

BEST TIMES TO VISIT

The coolest months, **May to September** have the most sunshine and least rain. Ideal weather for hiking, climbing and horse riding. The **November to March** summer rainy season is also very pleasant.

GETTING THERE

There are **light-aircraft** strips at Mutare, Nyanga and Chipinge. **Car hire** is available in Mutare, contact Europcar, tel: (120) 62304; Hertz, tel: (120) 64784. Daily **trains** run between Harare and Mutare, as does a daily **coach service** operated by Express Motorways, tel: (14) 720392. **Rural buses** operate between all the small centres. Otherwise, you will need a **car** to get to Nyanga, Bvumba or Chimanimani; the roads to all three areas are mostly tarred (gravel roads that do occur are accessible to passenger cars). For **minibus** travel from Mutare to Chimanimani, contact Eastern Tours, tel: (126) 294.

GETTING AROUND

A car is essential, although backpackers with patience will have no difficulty getting around. UTC (United Touring Company) arrange all-inclusive excursions to Bvumba and Nyanga from Mutare, tel: (120) 64784 or (14) 793701.

WHERE TO STAY

Nyanga
Troutbeck Inn: grand, overlooking lake, pine forests and mountain golf course, tel: (129-8) 305, or call Zimbabwe Sun, tel: (14) 736644.
Pinetree Inn near Juliasdale: English cottage-style hotel, best cream teas in the mountains, tel: (129) 25916.
Montclair Casino Hotel, Juliasdale: regular, multifacility holiday hotel, contact Zimbabwe Sun, tel: (14) 736644.
Rhodes Nyanga Hotel: Cecil John Rhodes' old farmstead, overlooks Rhodes Dam and distant hills, tel: (129-8) 377.

Cottage Accommodation
Many companies and individuals offer charming cottages in Nyanga; for details, call the Manicaland Publicity Association, tel: (120) 64711.

Mutare
Manica Hotel: the best, call Zimbabwe Sun, tel: (120) 64431.
Christmas Pass Hotel: tel: (120) 63818.
Wise Owl Motel: tel: (120) 64643.

Bvumba
Leopard Rock Hotel: lord of the mountains, sumptuous golfing resort and casino, La Roche restaurant excellent, tel: (120) 60115, fax: 791484.
White Horse Inn: genuine, small, owner-run inn; polished and professional, haute cuisine, tel: (120) 60325.
Inn on the Vumba, nearest to Mutare: recently refurbished, small, elegant, tel: (120) 60722.

The Castle: unique battlement guarding the keep to Leopard Rock, book months ahead for parties of up to six, tel: (120) 210320.

Private Cottages
Run by retired couples; the Manicaland Publicity Bureau regularly updates a list of some 10 cottages, tel: (120) 64711.

Chimanimani
Chimanimani Arms Hotel: old-world India, hill-country ambience; big double-storey hotel overlooks mountains; part of the lawns are available to campers, tel: (126) 511 or (14) 752125.
Hot Springs Resort, between Mutare and Chipinge: recommended, 12 thatched double lodges around lake, mineral spring pools, tel: (126) 361/7.

Chipinge
Chipinge Hotel: urban rustic, tel: (127) 2226.
Birchenough Bridge Hotel, near the Save River in the lowveld: rustic and hot, tel: (127) 225819.

BUDGET ACCOMMODATION
Nyanga
National Parks chalets at Udu, Rhodes, Pungwe drift (recommended) and Nyangwe (Mare); bookings must be made in Harare, tel: (14) 706077; also National Parks campsites at Nyangombe near Udu and at Mutarazi Falls, tel: (129-8) 384.

Eastern Highlands at a Glance

Mutare

Dandaro Lodge 7km (4 miles) from Mutare, near Penhalonga: in indigenous forested hills, tel: (120-5) 267.

La Rochelle near Penhalonga: National Trust property with a Norman tower, six chalets, tel: (120) 5250.

Backpackers' accommodation: at The Drifters private game park, will pick you up in Mutare, tel: (120) 62964.

Bvumba

National Parks campsite: excellent facilities at Bvumba Botanical Gardens, tel: (120) 212722; reservations must be made through central booking office, tel: (14) 706077, or pay when you arrive.

Chimanimani

Heaven Mountain Lodge: backpackers' dormitory for up to 20, dining room and lounge, tel: (126) 450 or 220.

Camping: campers allowed anywhere in the Chimanimani National Park, the mountain refuge hut near the Bundi River, and at Base Camp 19km (12 miles) from village, tel: (126) 5442; no caravans.

WHERE TO EAT

All hotels in Juliasdale, Nyanga, Troutbeck, Mutare, Bvumba, Chimanimani and Chipinge have restaurants.

Nyanga

Pine Tree Inn, Juliasdale: small, one of the best restaurants in the Eastern Highlands.

Village Inn: wholesome table d'hôte dinners in a family holiday atmosphere.

Rhodes Nyanga Hotel: smart-casual attire for a very reasonable six-course dinner.

Bvumba

Troutbeck Inn: book in advance, excellent selection of à la carte dishes and wines.

White Horse Inn: their cuisine is an art, book early.

La Roche, Leopard Rock Hotel: well-prepared, well-served meals of a standard high enough to satisfy most.

The Castle: honest, straightforward cooking (the chefs can also provide the culinary frills).

Chimanimani

Chimanimani Arms: old colonial feel, breakfasts are better than dinners.

TOURS AND EXCURSIONS

Birding safaris countrywide: run by Peter Ginn, photographer, bird-book writer and naturalist, tel: (179) 430017.

Horse riding: two-hour and full-day trails available from National Parks (Nyanga), tel: (129-8) 384; also at Leopard Rock Hotel and Troutbeck Inn.

Mountain walking and riding safaris in Nyanga: call Trails Unlimited, tel: (120) 63094.

Scenic day excursions: UTC offer a selection, tel: (120) 64784; for Eastern Highlands tours from Harare, call Rainbow Tours, tel: (14) 728303; or UTC, tel: (14) 793701.

Trout fishing: tackle available from Master Angler in Harare, fax: (14) 750525; flies from Kashmir Trading in Nyanga Village, tel: (129-8) 229.

Walking trails: Nyazengu's six nonguided trails start 5km (3 miles) from Nyangani Mountain car park; small fee payable on arrival at trout pools.

Wild-water kayaking and rafting on the Pungwe River: runs December through April, call Far and Wide Safaris, tel: (129) 26329; also rock-climbing, trout fishing, camping, hiking trails; the organization hires out mountain bikes, too, in Juliasdale.

USEFUL TELEPHONE NUMBERS

Automobile Association, tel: (120) 64422.

Manicaland Publicity Association, tel: (120) 64711.

National Parks central booking office, tel: (14) 706077.

Outward Bound School, tel: (126) 5440.

NYANGA	J	F	M	A	M	J	J	A	S	O	N	D
AVERAGE TEMP. °F	63	63	61	59	55	52	52	54	59	63	63	63
AVERAGE TEMP. °C	17	17	16	15	13	11	11	12	15	17	17	17
Hours of Sun Daily	6	6	7	8	8	8	8	9	9	9	7	6
RAINFALL ins.	10	10	6	2	1	1	1	0.5	1	2	5	10
RAINFALL mm	255	255	165	60	20	18	18	14	20	51	128	245
Days of Rainfall	19	18	16	9	5	5	5	4	2	7	12	19

8
Great Zimbabwe

The **Great Zimbabwe ruins**, of Roman proportions and the country's second World Heritage Site, is for many visitors Zimbabwe's greatest single attraction. Sited on an open wooded plain surrounded by hills, the ruins comprise the vast **Great Enclosure** complex, and on a nearby *kopje* the **Hill Complex**, a veritable castle of interlocking walls and granite boulders, while all around in the valley lie a myriad other walls. The ruins feature an array of chevron, herringbone and many other intricate patterns in its walls, and the astonishing fact is that despite the dry-stone technique used in Great Zimbabwe's construction (no mortar binds the stone blocks), the complex has endured for seven centuries. The whole covers an area of 720ha (1779 acres), the largest ruins complex in Africa. Home to perhaps 40,000 people when it was built in the 13th century, Portuguese traders, Victorian novelists such as Rider Haggard, and late 19th-century hunter–adventurers all added to the interpretation of the mystique of the ruins.

But it was the Rhodesians, particularly during the UDI (Unilateral Declaration of Independence) years, who really tried to rewrite history – even asserting that an African genesis for Great Zimbabwe was tantamount to treason. Fortunately, this is now behind the people of the country; today the great ruins represent the soul of the nation, the historical heritage of an empire after which today's Zimbabwe – meaning 'houses of stone' – is named, and both visitors and students can enjoy Great Zimbabwe in a spirit of awe and discovery worthy of it.

CLIMATE

Great Zimbabwe, at the edge of the central plateau, is high enough to enjoy **cooler temperatures** but with a touch of lowveld warmth. Its rainfall pattern is the same as the highveld, but it receives **less rain**. The rainy season occurs November through February while **June** and **July** are **cold, dry** months. A sweater or jacket for evenings is always a good idea.

Opposite: *The conical tower inside the Great Enclosure.*

DON'T MISS

*** Hill Complex; take refreshments and binoculars
*** Great Enclosure; walk along the narrow passage
** Great Zimbabwe Museum; contains fascinating finds
** Game-viewing on horseback
** Chapel of St Francis; try bellowing!
* Circular drive across the dam; great views
* Tea at the Great Zimbabwe Hotel
* Picnic at Mushandike Dam.

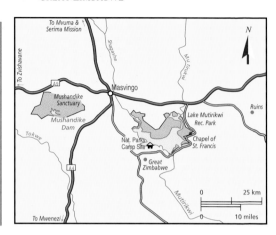

GREAT ZIMBABWE MUSEUM

Great Zimbabwe has suffered at the hands of light-fingered collectors over the centuries; amateur archaeologists have probed and in some cases, destroyed – which makes the Great Zimbabwe Museum a good place to start if one is interested in precious arte-facts. There is a nice walk-through display on the San hunter–gatherers (the original inhabitants of the area), which also shows the arrival of the first Iron Age people 1700 years ago. One can view the famous soapstone birds, possibly fish eagles, which were initially carried away by treasure hunters. Archaeologists believe the birds may be mythological, and they were probably part of the Hill complex, royal regalia and a small collection of oriental trade goods can also be seen.

THE MYSTERY OF GREAT ZIMBABWE

Wealthy cattlemen, the Shona-speaking ancestors of today's Zimbabweans, built Great Zimbabwe in the 13th and 14th centuries. Politicians and propagandists have long asserted that the origins of Zimbabwe are a mystery; speculation dwelt on the possibility of Phoenician, Arab, Indian or even ancient Hebrew influences. In fact, since archaeologist Gertrude Caton-Thompson's excavations in 1932, it has been widely known that Great Zimbabwe is truly of Africa and less than 1000 years old (although tour organizers do love a touch of the 'Temple of Doom'). Caton-Thompson's findings confirmed the work of Randall MacIver in 1906. Nearly all of Zimbabwe's artefacts are of local origin, and excavations at all levels record the remains of an African way of life. However, the old theories with their element of mystery take many years to die.

The Great Enclosure ★★★

The Great Enclosure, whose interlocking pieces of granite are 11m (36ft) high and 243m (797ft) in circumference, is the largest single ancient structure south of the Sahara. A monument of high, silent walls grey with lichen and redolent with 600 years of history, it embraces a chunky conical tower within, like a massive snuffbox.

The Enclosure represents the pinnacle of Shona architecture and the inspiration for some 150 other small *mazimbabwe* scattered throughout the country.

Inside, the king's family enjoyed their privacy in huts of polished *daga* (clay earth), pole and thatch. The perimeter wall is a substantial walk (an estimated million granite blocks may have been used to build it). Two high walls form a narrow passage giving direct access to the tower enclosure, and as one walks along it with the occasional grasping tree or eagle overhead, one understands the romanticism that gripped novel writers.

Archaeologists who dug beneath the conical tower, which has been likened to a symbolic grain store, found it to be solid right through. Similar smaller structures were found in the proliferation of valley ruins dividing the Enclosure from the Hill Complex. The tower has been carbon dated as one of the last structures to have been built at Great Zimbabwe, and again, there was no mortar used throughout. To some there is a similarity with the pillar tombs of the East African coast. Great Zimbabwe was undoubtedly the power point of an empire that covered much of southeast Africa.

> **MASVINGO**
>
> Masvingo means 'walled-in enclosure' and is Great Zimbabwe's town. A 13th-century Karanga king, Chikwagu, who resided at the Hilltop Complex, is thought to be responsible for some of the best of Great Zimbabwe's structures. Masvingo was called Fort Victoria for a while when elephant hunter Frederick Courtney Selous led Rhodes' pioneer column here in 1890. One of their 100-year-old towers still stands in the centre of town. Today Masvingo is essentially a petrol stop en route to Great Zimbabwe or South Africa. It has one of the country's only two ultracity-style gas stations and truck-ins.

The Hill Complex ***

In the parkland of trees between the Great Enclosure and the Hill Complex are acres of ruins where the more important notables first lived, with the ordinary people spreading out on the periphery; there are still remains of *daga* huts. These valley ruins, with the exception of the **Royal Treasury** excavated 120m (395ft) below the Great Enclosure, were built mainly in the later style, suggesting that the urban layout changed with increased population. There is a reconstructed **Karanga village** nearby.

Below: *Hilltop view of the Great Enclosure.*

The ruins of the Hill Complex are the oldest, and are divided into western and eastern halves. From a distance the bouldered hill rises some 80m (260ft) above the valley, well treed with euphorbias and *Brachystegia*. One side is a granite precipice. The entrance – there are three of them – is a long, walled, stepped ramp on the western side leading up to the huge snake-and-ladder walls where archaeologists dig and sift.

Balancing boulders blend with the intricate pattern of the stonework, and the view across the vast **Mutirikwi valley** to the lake is refreshing after the climb. The main perimeter wall is 5m (16ft) thick, and has proved to be a treasure trove of archaeological finds. It is believed that the hill ruins may have had significance as the spiritual and religious centre of the state, and that a special medium may have lived here.

Lake Mutirikwi *

The dam was built in 1961 to feed the vast lowveld sugar estates. In recent years, due to drought, it has seldom done its job. The National Parks wildlife area lies on the north bank of the Y-shaped 15km (9 miles) lake. A circular road, some 100km (60 miles), starts in Masvingo and leads around the lake and game reserve. In good years the waters are used for sailing, motorboating and bass fishing; there are also resident crocodile and hippo. Past the dam wall's concrete arch, the scenery across the Mutirikwi communal lands embraces high Scottish-like forested hills overlooking the expanse of water – perhaps the reason for the original name-givers calling it **Lake Kyle**, and the scenic drive, **Glenlivet**. Most of the leisure resorts are on the south bank near Great Zimbabwe. This area is often still simply called Kyle.

Lake Mutirikwi Recreational Park **

This recreational park (to distinguish it from a big Hwange-style national park) consists of the lake and a substantial game park on its twisting north bank. Here are the National Parks cottages and many kilometres of game trails, with names such as Rhino Peninsula, Buffalo Loop and Popoteke Picnic Site. Access is off the Masvingo–Birchenough Bridge road. National Parks provides mooring sites for boats at **Sikato Bay** near Great Zimbabwe. Most of the wildlife was introduced and includes white rhino,

kudu, oribi, wildebeest, nyala, buffalo, giraffe and many
species of antelope and bird. Look out for the miombo
rock thrush, collared sunbird and grey-headed gull; and
for the lanner falcon near the ruins. The habitat includes
miombo woodland, acacia thorn scrub and exposed
granite *dwalas*. Rock painting sites, particularly the
Chamavara cave, are accessible if you have a guide. The
horse trails led by rangers through the park are excellent.

Lakes by the Wayside: Ngezi and Mushandike ⋆

Between Harare and Masvingo there are two small
wildlife preserves, Ngezi and Mushandike, not normally
seen by visitors as they are off the beaten track. **Ngezi**, in
the eastern lea of the Mashava mountains, or **Great
Dyke**, is known for its summer fishing – and crocodiles.
Water-skiing is not allowed. The only four chalets, near
the dam wall and jetty, are set among rocky *Brachystegia*
trees, offering lovely sunset views. There is not a great
deal of game but walking is the best way to see it.

Mushandike's dam near Masvingo was built in 1938.
Here, in this steep *kopje* reserve with its tranquil lake, it is
possible in the dry season to lie on the long grassy banks
beneath shady trees. Only camping and caravan facilities
are available and, as always in Zimbabwe, a National
Parks attendant to help with the heavy chores.

Opposite: *A Shona village
in the rocky remoteness
of the 'middleveld' near
Masvingo.* **Left:** *Orna-
mental clay guinea fowl,
fashioned by rural folk for
the tourist trade.*

INTREPID TRAVELLERS

Until the development of railways in the 1890s, the principal method of transport in Africa was the ox wagon. In 1890, the first British to the country formed a *laager* near Great Zimbabwe to recuperate from the sweltering lowveld and to celebrate their escape from Ndebele *impis* who had shadowed them all the way. Later, Cecil John Rhodes brought up a number of black drivers from the mountain kingdom of Lesotho to help with transport, rewarding them with land where Mutirkwi Park now stands. Many of them died in the great flu epidemic of 1919; their graves, a few stone huts and a dam can be seen just off Nyala drive, 2km (1 mile) from the lodges.

Below: *Patient donkeys are still harnessed for farm work in the rural areas.*

Game-viewing on Horseback ★★

Whether a novice or expert, all are catered for at **Lake Mutirikwi** park (children under 10 must bring their own riding hats). Because the horse is able to go where a car cannot, the rider is able to draw physically and spiritually much closer to the game. A qualified ranger accompanies the group and will adjust saddle and stirrups for newcomers. The cost is low and rides last a few hours. Mutirikwi's wildlife was largely introduced, some from Kariba's Operation Noah (*see* p. 62); the white rhino breeding stock came from Natal. Although a small park by Zimbabwe's standards, it is one of the most populated wildlife areas in the country.

The Chapels ★★

The architectural magnificence of Great Zimbabwe may have inspired other designers. Near Masvingo on the Mutare road is the **Chapel of St Francis**, constructed by Italian prisoners of war during World War II, which has the remains of 71 soldiers who died in captivity in Zimbabwe. It is a simple, corrugated-roof building, but the interior is covered with paintings and simulated mosaics designed by the homesick soldiers. The wall murals were completed 10 years later by a number of Masvingo artists.

Serima Mission lies halfway between Mvuma and Masvingo, and 20km (12 miles) to the east via Chatsworth. Founded in 1948 by Swiss architect and priest Father John Groeber, its interior is a treasure house of carved African art. The church was built by the village community over three years; doors, beams and altar are all hand-carved. Like Cyrene Mission in Bulawayo and Driefontein Mission south of Masvingo on the Beitbridge road, it has contributed greatly to the fostering of local art.

Great Zimbabwe at a Glance

BEST TIMES TO VISIT

May to September are the coolest months. Rain can be consistent in December and January. Game-viewing is best **July to September**; October is also good but very hot.

GETTING THERE

United Air operates **weekly flights** from Harare to Masvingo; Air Zimbabwe handles the bookings, tel: (14) 575021. If travelling **by car**, a 26km (16 miles) tar access road commences just south of Masvingo.

GETTING AROUND

The choice is limited to **car hire**, joining a **package tour** or using your **own transport**. Car hire available from Hertz; contact them at Travelworld, tel: (139) 62131. Day-tour operators arrange **hotel pick-ups**, call United Touring Company (UTC), tel: (139) 62274 or 62131. Backpackers can catch the **Morgenster Mission bus** from the town centre. It goes via Great Zimbabwe to the mission south of the monument.

WHERE TO STAY

Great Zimbabwe Hotel: the only hotel near the ruins; small, with homely restaurant surrounded by bush, call hotel direct, tel: (139) 62274 or Zimbabwe Sun central booking office, tel: (14) 736644.
Msusu Safari Kraal: nice new lodge that's away from it all, tel: (14) 751331.

Kyle View Holiday Resort: has restaurant and pub, tel: (139) 7202.

National Parks Chalets
For choice accommodation, try the National Parks chalets on the north bank of Lake Mutirikwi, no meals, call central bookings, tel: (14) 706077, or the Mutirikwi park office, tel: (139) 62913.

Masvingo
Flamboyant Motel at Zimbabwe Ruins turnoff: the most comfortable, with old world touch, tel: (139) 62005.

BUDGET ACCOMMODATION
Self-catering lodges: on lake's south bank, contact Mutirikwe Lakeshore Lodges, tel: (139) 7151.
Camping: beautiful National Parks campsite at Sikato Bay, tel: (139) 7150.
Great Zimbabwe campsite: convenient, inexpensive; write to the Regional Director (Southern), PO Box 1060, Masvingo, or just arrive.

WHERE TO EAT

Great Zimbabwe Hotel serves adequate meals, but it is better, when visiting Great Zimbabwe, to always take a

picnic (although there is an attractive tearoom in the grounds near the curio and book shops).
The **Chevron** and **Flamboyant** hotels in Masvingo offer à la carte.
Fast-food outlets (Masvingo is not culinary corner): **Wimpy** at Riley's service station outside town, tel: (139) 64029.

TOURS AND EXCURSIONS

All-inclusive tours: several Harare-based operators offer tours to Great Zimbabwe, sometimes combined with other scenic destinations, call Rainbow Hotels and Tours, tel: (19) 733781; United Touring Company (UTC), tel: (14) 793701.
Game-viewing pony trails: call National Parks, tel: (139) 62913.

USEFUL TELEPHONE NUMBERS

Automobile Association, tel: (139) 62563.
Masvingo Publicity Association, tel: (139) 62643.
Prehistory Society of Zimbabwe, PO Box 867, Harare, tel: (14) 302385.
Wildlife Society of Zimbabwe, Mukuvisi Woodlands, tel: (14) 700451.

GREAT ZIMBABWE	J	F	M	A	M	J	J	A	S	O	N	D
AVERAGE TEMP. °F	73	72	70	68	61	57	55	61	66	72	73	73
AVERAGE TEMP. °C	23	22	21	20	16	14	13	16	19	22	23	23
Hours of Sun Daily	7	7	7	8	9	8	8	9	9	8	7	7
RAINFALL ins.	5	4.5	2	1	1	0	0	0	0.5	1	3	6
RAINFALL mm	146	117	68	25	12	6	2	3	10	26	89	154
Days of Rainfall	12	12	8	5	3	3	1	2	2	5	9	13

9
Gonarezhou
National Park

As of January 1994, **Gonarezhou** in Zimbabwe's southeast corner – hot, baobab wilderness country and the nation's second-largest game park – was once again fully functional and open to everyone after having been closed to the public for many years. The park is 150km (93 miles) long, and borders on Mozambique's game areas and South Africa's Kruger National Park, the three forming a natural migratory triangle for the animals. Although Gonarezhou is only a quarter the size of Kruger Park, its habitat is much wilder. These days, for the purposes of administration, it is divided into the northern Runde region (**Chipinda Pools**) and Mwenezi River (**Mabalauta Camp**) in the south.

Recent war in neighbouring Mozambique, poaching and a terrible drought prompted many to believe that Gonarezhou, 'place of elephant', was dying. But the park has proved them wrong – so much so that recently a surplus of 200 elephant (an amount beyond the park's carrying capacity) were translocated to Madikwe Reserve in South Africa, a distance of 1000km (621 miles). The operation was possibly the largest of its kind since Hannibal crossed the Apennines with elephant to defeat the Romans nearly 1700 years ago.

The relentless drought has undoubtedly left its mark: searing temperatures of 50°C (122°F) have caused the decimation of wildlife through starvation; good rains and tight management are needed for the park to fully recover. Nonetheless, Gonarezhou still holds its reputation as one of Zimbabwe's most unspoilt wilderness areas.

CLIMATE

Gonarezhou in the lowveld is **hot** and **semi-arid**. 70% of its **sparse rain** falls in the November to February **summer months**. A mild June and July winter leads to temperatures in excess of 40°C (104°F) in the summer. Much of the park is only 150m (492ft) above sea level.

Opposite: *Dramatic red-sandstone cliffs flank the Runde River that cuts through Gonarezhou.*

DON'T MISS

*** Pink Chilojo Cliffs at sunset on the Runde River
*** Machiniwa Pan; bird and wildlife
*** Runde–Save confluence; magnificent wilderness
** Chipinda Pools; hippo, Chivirira Falls
** Manjinji Pan for birds; ox-bow lake off the Mwenezi River
** Mwenezi River drive; pools, wildlife, Wright's Tower
* Gorhwana and Gorhwe pans; lovely bush drive
* Look out for the beautiful Star of the Save from May to September.

GONAREZHOU NATIONAL PARK
Chipinda Pools ***

The Runde River rises near the highveld town of **Gweru** and is part of the lowveld irrigation complex that enables the growing of Zimbabwe's petrol-blend sugar. Joined by the Chiredzi, its muddy and seasonal meanderings through forest banks, pans, baobabs and high cliffs rich in Africa's bird varieties provide the scenic focus for many of Gonarezhou's wildlife viewpoints (there is game, but unfortunately very little to be seen these days as a result of the recent drought). This is also the reason the river not always lives up to its name 'great floods'. But there are hippo aplenty – and they're very noisy at night. Upstream are the **Chivirira Falls**.

There are National Parks campsites at **Chipinda Pools** and **Chinguli**, and numerous others along the river, some excellent for fishing (access to which requires a four-wheel-drive vehicle). Although the river is navigable in parts, and at certain times of the year, boats are not permitted; nor is spear fishing. Rich in myth and Arab trader legend, the Runde lies in an endemic malarial area (make sure you take all the necessary precautions), but if you're interested in recapturing Courtney Selous and Wilbur Smith's Africa, pack up the Land-Rover and head for the river .

National Parks have a base and small ecological display near Chipinda Pools. Unlike much of Gonarezhou, Chipinda's campsite is open year-round and is the entrance point for the Runde–Save River portion of the park. A four-wheel-drive is not essential, but is handy on a sandy riverbed. The Chi-

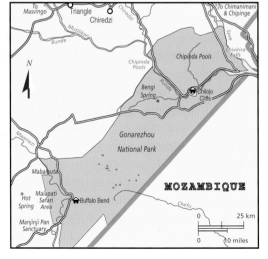

JUMBO TREK

Tender, loving care goes into the relocation of elephant to safer environments, as the following steps testify:
● Warden Clem Coetsee herds elephant by helicopter to waiting trucks, where they are darted with a morphine-based tranquillizer. A darted elephant has difficulty breathing, so Coetsee dangles from his chopper to free its trunk.
● Legs tied, the elephant is rolled by National Parks staff onto rubber mats.
● Winches haul the mat into a capture container where the elephant is revived with an antidote.
● Back on its feet, the elephant is coaxed into a linking 30-tonne truck which, to minimize separation trauma, contains the whole family. Water, food and TLC are administered before setting off.
● Poached-out herds as far north as Kenya may soon benefit from this revolutionary technique.

pinda and Chinguli campsites are well developed with ablution blocks, open dining rondavels and firewood is chopped by an attendant. There are another eight sites, including the spectacular **Chilojo Cliffs**, spread out along the length of the river.

You are left very much to yourself at all of these 'Out of Africa' hideaways (white tie for dinner is not obligatory!). The nearest supplies are at **Chiredzi**, the sugar town 41km (25 miles) distant.

Chilojo Cliffs ***

These cliffs, rising sheer from the blue, quiet pans of the Runde in layers of ochre, pink and orange, are part of a 32km (20 miles) sandstone massif visible from a great distance in Gonarezhou. They are one of the most startling features along the lazy river, especially when the sunset catches the fire in the stone. Baobabs, aloes and a variety of trees – dust-grey in the dry season – claw their way up to the base of the cliffs. It is an area rich in varied but not abundant wildlife (there are 57 species of mammal in Gonarezhou). Patience is needed as one waits beneath the canopy of nyalaberry and jackalberry trees at **Fishan's Camp** to spot some of the parading animals, from the more unusual suni antelope, white-striped nyala and Lichtenstein's hartebeest to elephant.

Above: *Lions are among Gonarezhou's predators. The varied wildlife in the park, and in particular, elephant, is best viewed around Chipinda Pools.*

Right: *The campsite at Chinguli, one of Gonarezhou's two public rest camps. There are also some delightful hides and picnic sites for those who prefer an even more intimate wilderness experience.*
Opposite: *The bloom of the Lowveld's lovely Save star, also known as impala lily.*

The cliffs represent the most recent sediment of what geologists call the 'chalk-deposit period', when much of Gonarezhou apparently faced a vast inland ocean. Gullies have worked their way through the cliffs, and the animals come down these to drink. On top of Chilojo Cliffs there are panoramic views of woodlands and mopane scrub – with the occasional mesa-like mountain rising from nowhere and the dry Runde riverbed snaking its way to the horizon.

The Rivers of Gonarezhou

The **Save**, Zimbabwe's largest internal river, begins its long journey to the Indian Ocean near the wine-farming area of Marondera. In the sweltering valley flanking the Chimanimani highlands, it is wide, with much soil erosion. On its banks live the most successful of Zimbabwe's log-hive wild honey farmers.

Passing under the spidery span of Birchenough Bridge, the Save is joined by the **Runde** at the easternmost spear of Gonarezhou National Park, the swamp wetland area that marks the border with Mozambique. The Save reaches the Indian Ocean south of Beira. Where the rivers join, the altitude is 90m (295ft), the lowest in Zimbabwe. The Save–Runde confluence is, during the rains, an exquisite water wonderland for birdwatchers, painters and poets.

SAUSAGE TREE

The sausage tree, with its huge fruit around 0.5m (1.5ft) long and weighing up to 10kg (22 lb), looks like a big oak with Christmas gifts tied to its branches. The tree grows to 18m (59ft), has distinct grey bark and dark maroon flowers whose smell is off-putting though loved by bats. The fruit is believed to contain an antidote cream for skin cancer. Although inedible, people continue to take it in various forms for rheumatism, ulcers, stomach ailments and syphilis. The seeds, when roasted, are eaten. The sausage tree is found along the banks of the Mwenezi River.

Machiniwa pan lies just east of the Runde with its winterthorn and dense riverine forest. There are water-birds and waders among the water lilies and reeds. In the lower Runde, as it flows into the Save, are tiny suni, large red fishing owl with their sepulchral screeching call and the colourful narina trogon bird, so named centuries ago by Frenchman François le Vaillant after his beautiful Khoisan lady. There is also the occasional and rare grand Mvule tree (*Chlorophora excelsa*). These days, the sandy rivers only flood for a few days each year. But there was a time when salt-water fish species from the Indian Ocean could be found in the river, among them the Zambezi shark, ox-eye tarpon and sawfish.

The boundary of the southern half of Gonarezhou, the area usually known as **Mabalauta**, is formed by the **Mwenezi**, a tributary of the Limpopo.

Mabalauta ★★

The National Parks offices are situated here, together with the nearby thatched **Swimuwini** chalets.

Mabalauta is Shangaan for the sandpaper-like fig-thicket tree, whose leaves can be used to sandpaper hides or hunting bows. Swimuwini refers not to any aquatic sport but means 'place of baobabs'; it is the park's main camp with chalets on a cliff overlooking the Mwenezi River's buffalo bend. Far below, the often-sandy river stretches in a languorous sweep to the distant haze.

From Swimuwini or Mabalauta the river flows southeast to the Limpopo border. North and south of the river are a series of viewpoints, pools and gorges – enough for days of exploring.

The area has a colourful history. Tonga–Hlengwe, and particularly Ndau-speaking folk – plus, of course, a few trans-Limpopo Venda – were some of the earlier inhabitants when General Soshangane and his Gaza *impis* stormed in during Shaka Zulu's

> **STAR OF THE SAVE**
>
> In the Yemen, where it was first identified, this succulent was known as the many-flowered plant. It is also called the Sabi star, impala lily – and part of its Latin name *Adenium obesum* hints at its chubby, baobab-like trunk, most of which is underground. It grows in Gonarezhou, flowering from May to September. The shrub, covered in white, pink-edged, star-shaped flowers, likes rocky areas and is the leading lady of the lowveld floral line-up. Like its sister, the Runde star, it is specially protected in Zimbabwe.

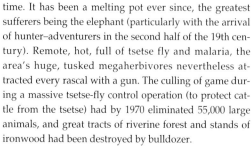

POOLS OF THE GAME

• **Samalema**, 'place of execution', is a gorge pitted with pools and potholes.
• **Malokwani Pool**: here the Mukwakwa, or Shangaan wild orange – which has a woody shell for painting and carving – can be eaten.
• **Mwatombo Pools** has a shelter against a rock face; below, deep sombre pools.
• **Rossi Pools** viewpoint, a secluded National Parks campsite, is high above the river and named after missionary Father Rossi who loved the area.
• **Wright's Tower** was built by conservationist Allan Wright (author of *Valley of the Ironwoods*), who was district commissioner of the Mwenzi area for 10 years and did much to make Gonarezhou a national park.

time. It has been a melting pot ever since, the greatest sufferers being the elephant (particularly with the arrival of hunter–adventurers in the second half of the 19th century). Remote, hot, full of tsetse fly and malaria, the area's huge, tusked megaherbivores nevertheless attracted every rascal with a gun. The culling of game during a massive tsetse-fly control operation (to protect cattle from the tsetse) had by 1970 eliminated 55,000 large animals, and great tracts of riverine forest and stands of ironwood had been destroyed by bulldozer.

The recent civil war in Mozambique further exacerbated the situation. But the park itself, free of poachers, war and old-fashioned ideas of cattle protection (today, game farming has turned out to be far more profitable than cattle), is still a magnificent spot.

Plain and Pan **

Ironwood, between the Mwenzi River and the Zimbabwe rail line which cuts through the park en route to Mozambique, is one of several pans to which the animals come to drink. Others radiate out from the river alongside gravel roads, some of which are accessible by car, though only a bakkie or a four-wheel-drive-vehicle will reach all of them. They include the **Manyanda Pan** (place of honey-eating hunters) with its viewing platform, **Mafuku** and **Lipakwa** off Soshangane Drive.

Below: *Touring Gonarezhou by four-wheel-drive.*

The ironwood – an extremely valuable tree – is termiteproof and smells of honey when it is cut. At **Ironwood viewpoint** on the Mwenzi on a clear day, one can see Crooks Corner and look across to Mozambique.

Beyond the lonely railway are the even wilder and more remote **Gorhwe and Gorhwana Pans**, some 15 of them dotted across this vast expanse of bushveld.

Gonarezhou National Park at a Glance

BEST TIMES TO VISIT

The dry season months, **May** to **October**, are the best (but from September, very hot). During the sparse rains, the National Parks camps at Chipinda Pools and Mabalauta are also open, but travel on game-viewing roads is restricted; prior advice should be sought from National Parks.

GETTING THERE

United Air usually operates several flights weekly from Harare, via Masvingo, to **Buffalo Range airport** in Triangle–Chiredzi; call Air Zimbabwe for reservations, tel: (14) 575021. Northern Gonarezhou is approached **by road** via Chiredzi, while the south is reached via Rutenga off the Beitbridge–Harare highway. The gravel road between the two is for four-wheel-drive vehicles only.

WHERE TO STAY

National Parks has chalets at **Swimuwini** and many campsites in both sectors of the park, some with ablution facilities and attendants. Caravans are permitted at **Chipinda Pools**. Prebook accommodation through National Parks, tel: (14) 706077.

Luxury safari lodges
Recommended (among the country's best) on the northern Gonarezhou border are: **Induna Lodge**, on Lone Star Safari Ranch: tucked in craggy gorge facing a lake, wildlife includes the 'big five', contact Wilderness Safaris, tel: (113) 4527.
Mahenye Wilderness Lodge and **Chilo Lodge**: the first on a Save River island, the other high on a Save cliff; eco-friendly units spectacularly remote in keeping with the rugged surroundings, call Zimbabwe Sun, tel: (14) 736644.

Accommodation en route from Beitbridge:
Lion and Elephant Motel, Bubye River: hugs the banks of the dry river, old-fashioned breakfasts; popular stop-off point on way to Harare, write to PO Box 148, Beitbridge; tel: (114) 2602.
Threeways Safaris, Bubye River: Hemingway country; river-bank chalets, paraffin lamps and home cooking; write to PO Box 49, Beitbridge; tel: ask operator for Rutenga (code 114), then ask for 01320.

En route from Harare, Mutare and Bulawayo
Great Zimbabwe Hotel: tel: (139) 62274.
Chimanimani Arms: tel: (126) 511.
Tambuti Lodge Motel, Chiredzi: tel: (131) 2575.

Planters Inn, Chiredzi: tel: (131) 2281.
Or try the following two conservancies:
Save Valley Wildlife Conservancy game ranch, call Zimbabwe Sun, tel: (131) 252924.
Chiredzi Wildlife Conservancy game ranch, tel: (131) 2865.

WHERE TO EAT

There are no hotels or restaurants in Gonarezhou. Visitors should come fully equipped.

TOURS AND TRIPS

Horse safaris near Gonarezhou: contact Biza Saddle Safaris, tel: (14) 45752.
Photographic safaris: available through Induna Lodge and Zimbabwe Sun safari lodges, *see* listings above.
Wilderness walking trails: National Parks operate three-to-six-day trails in Gonarezhou, tel: (14) 706077.

USEFUL TELEPHONE NUMBERS

Lone Star Ranch manager, tel: (131) 236925.
National Parks central booking office, tel: (14) 706077.
National Parks (Mabalauta and Swimuwini), tel: (131) 2980.

GONAREZHOU	J	F	M	A	M	J	J	A	S	O	N	D
AVERAGE TEMP. °F	72	70	69	66	59	54	54	59	66	70	72	70
AVERAGE TEMP. °C	22	21	21	19	15	12	12	15	19	21	22	21
Hours of Sun Daily	8	7	8	8	9	9	9	9	9	8	8	7
RAINFALL ins.	5	4	2	1	0	0	0	0	0	1.5	4	5
RAINFALL mm	134	97	50	28	7	2	1	1	8	36	99	131
Days of Rainfall	11	9	6	4	1	1	1	0	0	1	4	9	11

10
Bulawayo and Matobo National Park

The *amatobo* or 'bald-headed hills', as Mzilikazi, Zulu warlord and founder of the amaNdebele nation, called them, are in fact very old: over 3000 million years. This moonscape of endless granite humpbacks covers a huge area south of Zimbabwe's second city, **Bulawayo**. The most spectacular section is the **Matobo National Park**, with painted caves, wildlife, dams and the **World's View** grave of Cecil John Rhodes.

The **Matobo Hills** have been inhabited for 40,000 years – first by the San hunter–gatherers, later the Torwa (architects of beautiful Kame), and then by Changamire and his Rozvi, who were finally edged out by the Zulus. Mzilikazi was one of many fine warriors who, to escape Shaka's mania, stormed out of Zululand in the early 19th century. After being forced north across the Limpopo by the Voortrekkers, he eventually settled at N'tabazinduna, there to divide his conquered lands among his regiments and *induna* favourites. The demise of the Ndebele as a warrior nation took place between 1893 and 1897 with the arrival of the white colonists during the time of Lobengula (Mzilikazi's son). Shield, assegai and rifle were no match for the hard-eyed horsemen with machine guns. Lobengula fled his capital, guBulawayo, and the Ndebele were methodically annihilated, though the white settlers also suffered casualties.

The surrounding hills and plains, conflict focus of Shona dynasties, Ndebele armies and British colonists, are redolent with history, myth and the memories of a thousand battles that once reverberated within them.

CLIMATE

Zimbabwe's lowest temperature of -11°C (12°F) in 1972 was recorded in the Matobo Hills. Lying close to the Kalahari thirstlands, it is **very dry**. It has one of the lowest rainfall figures of all Zimbabwe's wilderness areas (excluding Gonarezhou), although the months **November through February** experience major **downpours**. Its altitude ameliorates the worst year-end summer heat.

Opposite: *The Matobo Hills are famed for their massive boulders and balancing rocks.*

DON'T MISS

*** World's View (Malindi-dzimu); panoramic view from Cecil Rhodes' grave site
*** Matobo National Park; lovely scenic drives (and, even better, pony trails)
** Painted Caves; greatest concentration of San rock art in Zimbabwe
** Kame Ruins; largest, after Great Zimbabwe, of 150 similar ruins
** Natural History Museum; you will spend hours here
** Railway Museum; venerable locomotives
* Mzilikazi Art and Craft Centre; watch potters and stone sculptors at work
* Chipangali; hundreds of orphaned animals.

INTERESTING FACTS ON OLD BULAWAYO

• The State House is on the site of King Lobengula's *kraal*; the *indaba* (meeting) tree still stands in the gardens.
• Bulawayo Club features colonnades, and lining the street outside, flamboyants introduced from Madagascar.
• The City Hall, with its curio sellers, palms and publicity bureau, is the site of the 1896 *laager*; the well sunk by the first Europeans to visit Bulawayo is still there.
• The High Court boasts Grecian columns and a green St Peter's cupola.
• The Railway Station, with tiny shops nearby and furtive forex dealers, was in 1898 part of the Cape-to-Cairo dream rail line.

BULAWAYO

Bulawayo, which means 'place of slaughter', is for Western visitors a more attractive city than Zimbabwe's capital, Harare. Many of its old British colonial buildings still stand in streets broad enough for an ox wagon to turn around in; and together with its fleet of almost-vintage cars and air of *déjà vu*, the setting makes it magic for movies. *Cry Freedom*, the prestigious *A World Apart* and *The Power of One* were all partly filmed in Bulawayo.

Steeped in history, attractions include the ancient ruins of **Kame** (a half-day trip) and the **Matobo Hills** (worth a full day's visit); within the city limits are the country's **Natural History Museum**, and its railway system that includes steam locomotive yards and a museum of old trains and coaches dating back to 1896. Animal lovers can visit the **Tshabalala** game sanctuary (*see* p. 116), and the **Chipangali Wildlife Orphanage** (23km, or 14 miles, outside Bulawayo on the Beitbridge road) where sick and abandoned animals (big cats, too) are cared for.

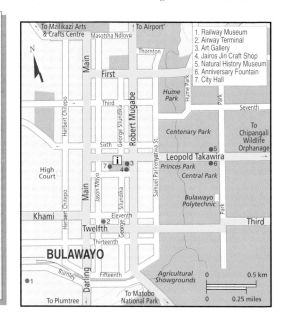

1. Railway Museum
2. Airway Terminal
3. Art Gallery
4. Jairos Jiri Craft Shop
5. Natural History Museum
6. Anniversary Fountain
7. City Hall

Steam Train Safari ★★

A journey by steam train is rare today; however, National Railways of Zimbabwe still operate a fleet of these romantic passenger locomotives on behalf of a company called Rail Safaris. The most common is the 20A Class Garratt, but they also run a 15th Class Garratt articulated steam-locomotive of 1952 vintage. This belching monster is used monthly on the Bulawayo-based Zambezi Special rail safari. Sumptuous 1920s emerald-and ivory-class coaches afford elegant game-viewing as the train crosses Hwange Park on its way to Victoria Falls, the end of the journey.

The Railways operate an open-air vintage train museum in Bulawayo that includes nine steam locos (the earliest, Jack Tar, was built in 1896), a 1904 museum coach and Rhodes' 1896 Pullman saloon that was used to bring his body from Cape Town to the Matobo Hills.

A Booth travelling crane first used in Beira in 1913, a 1907 Pickering livestock wagon and a 1931 tin-roofed

Above: *Tree-garlanded scene outside the old-established Bulawayo Club.*

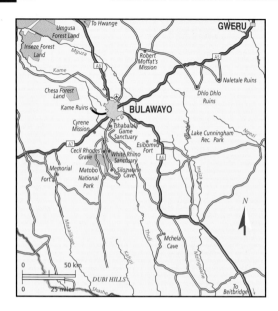

country railway station – with original fire buckets, rain gauge, lamps and notice boards – complete the exhibit. The museum is on Prospect Avenue, off Josiah Chinamano Road, in the Raylton suburb. Ask for permission and directions to the fiendish steam-loco maintenance sheds as well; call the Railway Historical Committee for further information.

MATOBO NATIONAL PARK

Still often referred to as the Matopos, the Matobo range encompassing the national park is a rugged wilderness of soaring black eagles, caves, rain-streaked *dwala* (whale-back mountains), Bushman rock paintings, leopard, rainbow-coloured lizards and hiking grandeur.

The chaotic weather-cracked hills, spiritual home of the Rozvi mediums, are divided into five wilderness areas: the northern area encompassing **World's View**, Togwe in the east with its **Inanke Cave** paintings, **Maleme Dam** and holiday chalets in the centre, and further west, the actual game park in the Whovi wilderness. The south is known as the Maleme wilderness area.

Surrounding the Matobo Park are a wealth of treasures: the **Bambata Caves**, **Cyrene Mission**'s decorated dwellings, and **Fort Usher**, where Lord Baden-Powell conceived his idea of the Boy Scout movement. It is also the spot where Rhodes held his peace *indaba* with the Ndebele elders 100 years ago. Mzilikazi, founder of the Ndebele nation, is buried in these hills, his memorial plaque weathered by time. 'Bull elephant' and 'warrior king' were some of the praises attributed to him.

TSHABALALA GAME SANCTUARY

One of King Mzilikazi's many wives, a Swazi woman named Fulata from the Tshabalala clan, gave birth to Lobengula, a man destined to be king. One of his daughters married Englishman Fairburn Usher (nicknamed Pondwene), a sailor who lived as an Ndebele on Tshabalala in 1883. Tshabalala became a National Parks game sanctuary in 1978. Similar in a way to Mukuvisi Woodlands in Harare, it offers walking and horse trails, picnic sites, small game and bird-watching. The sanctuary lies 11km (7 miles) from Bulawayo on the Matobo Hills road.

Recent developments in the park include the establishment of several luxury safari lodges on its fringes,
among them Matobo Hills, Amalinda and Zindele.

World's View ***

Known to the Shona Karanga, who occupied these hills
prior to the Ndebele, as the 'high place of the *midzimu*
spirit elders', Malindidzimu was in turn described by
Rhodes with some understatement as 'one of the world's
views'. It lies 45km (28 miles) south of Bulawayo in the
Matobo National Park.

Massive balls of stone form a natural amphitheatre
surrounding the hilltop grave of this charismatic imperi-
alist. There is nothing elaborate about it: simple, austere,
the bald inscription in bronze is cut into the granite at
one's feet. Falling away on all sides is a giant's playground of knuckled hills, Kipling's ancient granite of the
north – ridge after ridge to the fiery horizon.

The Painted Caves **

The belief in *Mwari*, the supreme being, was a cohesive
religious force at Great Zimbabwe. Continued under the
Rozvi dynasty, *Mwari Matonjeni* was the great spirit of
the Matobo Hills. Shrine oracles in many a cave were
consulted by elders, especially when the need for rain –

Left: *The grave of Cecil
John Rhodes – Kipling's
'immense and brooding
spirit' – atop World's View.*

source of all life for rural people – was urgent. The oracles were often older women who spoke as the voice of *Mwari* from the gloomy depths of a cave.

During Mzilikazi's time, instead of trying to eradicate this aspect of Shona culture, the Ndebele had the good sense not only to allow its continuation, but to regularly consult the oracles themselves. *Mwari* shrines in Matobo include *Matonjeni* and *Mjelele*.

Up to 40,000 years before the Torwa, Rozvi or Ndebele came to the Matobo caves, however, they were occupied by San hunter–gatherers.

At least five caves are well documented today. At **Pomongwe Cave** there is a site museum where thousands of unearthed Stone Age implements and Iron Age artefacts are on display. In the 1920s, a covering of oil and glycerine was applied to the cave's paintings that not only failed to preserve them, but came close to destroying the giraffe, zebra, antelope and human figures. Stone scrapers dating back to 7500BC have been unearthed in the ash, known as the Kame layer, as well as other deposits carbon dated to 14,000BC.

Nswatugi Cave with its interpretive display has excellent paintings, particularly of kudu and giraffe. The **White Rhino Shelter** has outline painting, **Bambata** is the most excavated, while the art at **Inanke** achieves a perfection of prehistoric complexity, skill and beauty. **Silozwane**, just south of the park, contains a fascinating range of domestic scenes. A series of painted arrows leads you to the cave's paintings, one of which depicts a giraffe standing 2m (6.5ft) high, and a snake that has an antelope's head.

Below: *The caves and cliffs of the Matobo area provide the 'canvas' for a myriad prehistoric rock paintings, many of superb quality.*

Kame Ruins **

Built by the Torwa dynasty in the 17th and 18th centuries, Kame – meaning 'home of kings' – represents a more sophisticated development of the Great Zimbabwe tradition of construction. Lying 22km (15 miles) west of Bulawayo, it is a national monument. Hunter–gatherers lived here up to 200,000 years ago.

When Great Zimbabwe collapsed, the Torwa state moved to this site on a hill above the river and made it their capital. Once again, dry-stone building techniques were utilized. The *mambo* ruler's personal hill complex was accessed via a series of rising walled platforms of chequered design, on which were built *pole-and-daga* huts. Spears, ivory charms, soapstone pipe bowls for smoking, copper items and rulers' traditional black-and-red patterned drinking pots have been excavated from what used to be an ivory-tusked passageway.

South of the hill complex, near the car park, is a carved Tsoro game board rather like Chinese chequers; it is still played throughout Zimbabwe.

Danangombe (also called Dhlo Dhlo) and **Naletale** are handsome ruins, too, an hour and a half's drive from Bulawayo, in the Matabeleland area.

Above: *The Naletale ruins are noted for the intricate herringbone, chequered and chevron patterns carved into the stonework. Naletale is one of a great many ancient structures in Zimbabwe; some have yielded golden bangles, beads and other African artefacts together with treasures of Portuguese origin, among them silver chalices and candlesticks, seals, medallions and bowls.*

Bulawayo and Matobo National Park at a Glance

The **June–July** winter months are always the best (this applies to Zimbabwe as a whole); **April** and **September** are also good. Matobo is drier than a lot of the country, although February has an average of one day's rain in three.

Direct **road**, **coach**, **rail** and **air** connections to Bulawayo from Botswana, Johannesburg, Victoria Falls and Harare. Coach companies to contact are Mini-Zim Travel (luxury minicoach service between South Africa and Zimbabwe), tel: (19) 76645, or, for Express Motorways, call UTC, tel: (19) 61402.

Public transport is limited. **Taxis** are available; for **car hire**, try Europcar, tel: (19) 67925, also Avis, Hertz, Mimosa; for **bicycle** (and car) hire, Transit, tel: (19) 76495. **Rural buses** from Bulawayo's Mzilikazi Police Station terminus operate to all the small centres in and around Bulawayo. **Urban buses** depart from City Hall (publicity bureau) terminus. You will need your **own car** for the Matobo National Park, or take a **safari company tour**.

Bulawayo
The city has five good hotels:
Bulawayo Holiday Inn: recently renovated, near Ascot racecourse, quiet and not too big, tel: (19) 72164.
Bulawayo Sun Hotel: central, business favourite, tel: (19) 60101.
Cresta Churchill, 6km (4 miles) out of town: Elizabethan beams and copper, cosy pub, tel: (19) 41016.
The Nesbitt Castle in Hillside suburb: this Macbeth-like fortress has period décor, baronial rooms and sumptuous prices, tel: (19) 42726.
Induna Lodge: African safari in the suburbs, tel: (19) 45684.

En route to Matobo from Beitbridge
Barbeton Lodge, southwest of West Nicholson: hilltop lodge in Bubyana black rhino conservancy; 10 linked ranches, 129,500ha (320,000 acres) with hippo, sable and elephant; for directions, tel: (19) 64638, fax: 72870.
Todds Hotel, West Nicholson: comfortable and friendly wayside inn, tel: (116) 5403.

Matobo National Park
National Parks lodges (Fish Eagle, Black Eagle and others) at Maleme Dam: beautiful setting on rocky promontories with lovely views, tel: (19) 63646 or ask for Matobo, then (0) 1913.
Chalets: One- and two-roomed; outside cooking and communal ablution facilities.
Camping and caravanning: facilities at five scenic sites, where you should ensure that all water is boiled; call National Parks, tel: (14) 706077.

Luxury Safari Lodges
Malalangwe, an hour from Bulawayo on Francistown road: seven luxury double cottages at Marula; historic and photographic tours a speciality, tel: (19) 74693.
Matobo Hills, just outside park near World's View: one of three best lodges in Zimbabwe (part of Touch the Wild safari group), local culture tours, tel: (19) 74589.
Shumba Shaba, 50km (31 miles) from Bulawayo on Mzilikazi Memorial road near Matobo Mission: four lodges run by Zindele Safaris, tel: (19) 64128.
Amalinda, off the main road to Matobo National Park, not far from Bambata Caves wild area: rocky, rugged setting, run by Londa Mela Safaris, tel: (19) 41286.
Izintaba, near Marula: four chalets for eight people in bushveld, 40 species of game, tel: (19) 69829.
N'tabazinduna (hill of the chiefs), on a farm 15km (9 miles) from Bulawayo: has a swimming pool, tel: (19) 26011.
Note: Almost all of the above have wildlife, and specialize in local and countrywide photographic game safaris.
There are nine safari-operated lodges within 100km (60 miles) of Bulawayo, with two in West Nicholson (172km, or

Bulawayo and Matobo National Park at a Glance

107 miles, from Bulawayo); contact Bulawayo Publicity Association, tel: (19) 60867.

BUDGET ACCOMMODATION

Hilltop Motel, 5km (3 miles) along Johannesburg road: lovely pool-braai area among the trees, tel: (19) 72493.

Backpackers and the budget-conscious should try:
Eland Grey's Inn, tel: (19) 60121.
Inungu Guest House, near Matobo National Park, tel: (19) 67791.
Bulawayo Municipal Camp Site, chalets also available, tel: (19) 63851.

WHERE TO EAT

There are no restaurants or shops in the Matobo National Park, although Fryers Store is 10km (6 miles) from Maleme Dam; call operator and ask for Matobo, then (0) 0112. The nearby safari lodges all have restaurants, although they are not normally available for guests passing through.

Bulawayo

Massimo's, Ascot Cntr, Leopold Takawira and Johannesburg roads: Italian, the best in Bulawayo (possibly in the country), tel: (19) 67430.
New Orleans: chic bayou atmosphere (the owners also run Banff Lodge nearby), tel: (19) 43176.
Cattleman Steakhouse: fast steaks, tel: (19) 76086.

Peking Restaurant: good, occasionally excellent, Chinese meals, tel: (19) 60646.

TOURS AND EXCURSIONS

Archaeology and palaeontology safaris (around Beitbridge and South African border): Limpopo Safaris, tel: (186) 43521.
Bulawayo circular self-drive: try the following route: Mbembezi battle memorial, N'tabazinduna execution spot, Danangombe and Naletale ruins, Inyati mission of Robert Moffat; the Jabulani safari lodges are nearby, tel: (150) 232. Contact Bulawayo Publicity Association for further ideas, tel: (19) 60867.
Chipangali Wildlife Orphanage: recommended, self-drive or contact any of the tour companies listed below, tel: (19) 70764.
Mzilikazi Art and Craft Centre, Mzilikazi suburb: free guided tours, tel: (19) 67245.
N'tabazinduna trails: historical trails, tel: (19) 26110.
Pony trails: contact Matobo National Park's office for following-day bookings, tel: (183-8) 2504, or ask for Matobo, then (0) 1913.
Ranch hunting: several ranches in the Bulawayo area offer ranch hunt facilities and accommodation; check with the Zimbabwe Association of Tour and Safari Operators in Harare, tel: (14) 733211, fax: 723230.
Steam-train safaris: highly recommended, contact Rail Safaris, tel/fax: (19) 75575.
Tailormade tours (city tours, Matobo National Park, Kame): Black Rhino Safaris, tel: (19) 41662; UTC (United Touring Company), tel: (19) 61402; Africa Dawn Safaris, tel: (19) 46696; Shishona Safaris, tel: (19) 76260.

USEFUL TELEPHONE NUMBERS

Automobile Association, tel: (14) 70063.
Bulawayo Publicity Association, Town Hall, Fife St between Leopold Takawira and Eighth Ave, tel: (19) 60867, fax: 60868.
Railway Historical Committee, tel: (19) 363318.
Zimbabwe Association of Tour and Safari Operators and **Professional Hunters and Guides Association**, tel: (14) 733211, fax: 723230.
Tshabalala Game Sanctuary, tel: (19) 43411.
Wildlife Society of Zimbabwe, Mukuvisi Woodlands, tel: (14) 700451.

BULAWAYO	J	F	M	A	M	J	J	A	S	O	N	D
AVERAGE TEMP. °F	72	72	70	66	63	57	57	63	68	72	72	72
AVERAGE TEMP. °C	22	22	21	19	17	14	14	17	20	22	22	22
Hours of Sun Daily	7	7	8	8	9	9	9	10	9	9	7	7
RAINFALL ins.	5	4	2	1.5	0	0	0	0	0	1.5	4	5
RAINFALL mm	134	104	52	38	8	2	1	2	8	35	96	128
Days of Rainfall	12	11	4	4	2	1	1	1	1	5	10	13

Travel tips

Tourist Information

The **Zimbabwe Tourist Board** has offices in South Africa (Johannesburg), the USA (Chicago), the United Kingdom (London), Germany (Frankfurt), and Switzerland (Zürich). The Tourist Board's head office is in Tourism House, 105 Jason Moyo Avenue, corner Fourth Street, Causeway, Harare; PO Box 8052, Causeway, Harare; tel: (14) 793666/7/8. **Publicity bureaus** are based in Bulawayo (Matobo), tel: (19) 60867; Harare, tel: (14) 705085; Great Zimbabwe, tel: (139) 62643; Mutare, tel: (120) 64711; and Victoria Falls, tel: (113) 4202.

The **National Parks and Wildlife Management** headquarters are in the Botanical Gardens, Borrowdale Road/Sandringham Drive, Harare; PO Box 8365, Causeway, Harare; for reservations, tel: (14) 726089 or 706077. There is also an office in Bulawayo, tel: (19) 63646. The **Wildlife Society of Zimbabwe** as well as the **Zambezi Society** are situated in the Mukuvisi Woodlands,

Glenara Avenue South, Harare. The Wildlife Society's postal address is PO Box 4665, Highlands, Harare; tel: (14) 731596. For the Zambezi Society, write to PO Box UA 334, Union Avenue, Harare. To contact the **Zimbabwe Association of Tour and Safari Operators** (ZATSO) and **Zimbabwe Professional Hunters and Guide Association**, call (14) 733211, fax: 723230; for ZATSO in Bulawayo, tel: (19) 730771.

Entry Requirements

All visitors need a passport that is valid for at least six months; very few require visas. Visitors should check with the Zimbabwean diplomatic mission in their country, or contact the Chief Immigration Officer at PB 7717, Causeway, Harare, tel: (14) 791913. Any Air Zimbabwe office will be able to help too. You will also require either a return air ticket, your own car or sufficient travel cheques to be able to continue your journey. Zimbabwe is a convenient place to obtain visas for other African countries.

Health Requirements

The climate is high, dry and healthy. Malaria, bilharzia and AIDS are, however, hazards in Zimbabwe. Travellers from South Africa or coming direct from Western countries need no inoculations at all. There is no malaria on the highveld. Water can be drunk from any tap in the cities and in most visitor areas. Zimbabwe was the third country in the world to screen donated blood for AIDS (a few months ahead of the UK). Always take precautions against the persistent overhead sun. In the winter months, the big-game areas can be dusty.

Travel

Harare and Victoria Falls are the main entry points by air. Harare is serviced by carriers from South Africa, Europe, Australia and a variety of African countries.
Customs: Five litres of liquor may be brought in, two of which may be spirits. All monies brought in should be declared on a forex form in order to guarantee its re-export. Importing a pet is very

difficult; you need to write to the Director of Veterinary Services, PO Box 8012, Causeway; tel: (14) 791355.

Road Travel
A superb road network connects Zimbabwe with all its neighbours, making it possible to drive from Cape Town, Windhoek, Beira, Gaborone, Blantyre, Lusaka or Nairobi. Rail connections are almost as good. The roads linking the cities with Victoria Falls, Hwange Game Reserve and the Eastern Highlands are all good tar roads. Hitchhiking is fine. Access to Matusadona, Chizarira, Mana Pools and Gonarezhou should only be undertaken in four-wheel-drive vehicles (although some incredible sedan journeys have been recorded).

Driver's licence: Always carry your licence with you, which should have a photo on it.

Road rules: In Zimbabwe, one drives on the left and gives way to the right. The speed limit on open roads is 100kph (60mph). A 'robot' is a traffic light. Drive defensively; city drivers, especially emergency taxis, will pull over suddenly to pick up passengers. Long-distance rural buses are equally reckless.

Car hire: Companies including Europcar, Hertz and Avis are well represented. Petrol and diesel are available at prices somewhat less than in South Africa or the UK.

Automobile Association: Membership of the AA is desirable; the main office is located at Fanum House,

Samora Machel Avenue, Harare; tel: (14) 752779. There are AA representatives in most of Zimbabwe's cities.

Maps
The AA produces a good map. More detailed ones are available from the Government Surveyor at Electra House, Samora Machel Avenue, Harare; tel: (14) 794545. City maps of Harare and Bulawayo are sold in book stores.

Coach travel: Coach services (semiluxury) link the main centres. Try Express Motorways, tel: (14) 720392, or Ajays, tel: (14) 703421.

Clothes: What to Pack
Lightweight clothing in neutral colours is suitable for the bush (including a long-sleeved shirt and long pants against mosquitoes in the evenings). Pack a hat, sunglasses and strong shoes for walking. You'll need a warm jacket for winter evenings. The occasional city restaurant may require smart-casual dress and even a tie. Take a raincoat for the Victoria Falls rain forest.

Books to Bring
Roberts' Birds of Southern Africa, Newman's Birds of Southern Africa and *Sasol Birds of Southern Africa* (all published in South Africa). The *Bundu* series, published in Zimbabwe, covers every wildlife subject; for example: *Birds of the Highveld* by Peter Ginn, and *Snakes of Zimbabwe* by D.G. Bradley and E.V. Cook.

Land Mammals of Southern Africa (a field guide) by Reay H.N. Smithers, published in South Africa.
Wild Flowers of Zimbabwe by D.C.H. Plowes and R.B. Drummond.
Rhodesian Wild Flowers by Margaret H. Tredgold.
Trees of Southern Africa by Keith Coates Palgrave.

Money Matters
The Zimbabwe dollar is divided into 100 cents. Notes are in denominations of Z$20, Z$10, Z$5 and Z$2; coins in 1c, 5c, 10c, 20c, 50c and Z$1.

Currency exchange: Money can be exchanged at hotels, banks or bureaux de change. Until recently there was a flourishing black market in currency, but with market liberalizaton, this has all but disappeared as there is sufficient forex available through normal channels.

Banks: Normal banking hours are 08:30 to 13:30 on weekdays (Wednesdays 13:00) and on Saturdays, 08:30 to 11:30.

Credit cards are International credit cards are acceptable, particularly at hotels and restaurants, but not every shop is used to them, especially in the smaller centres.

Tipping: Tip practically everywhere, it's much appreciated (around 10%).

Accommodation
Hotels are graded one to five stars (somewhat overoptimistically in the higher ranges). The service is often superlative. The largest and most expensive are the **Zimbabwe**

Sun hotels, tel: (14) 736644, followed by **Cresta Hotels**, tel: (14) 703131 or 751085, and **Rainbow Hotels**, tel: (14) 7337871. Among the most luxurious of the big hotels are Meikles in Harare, the Victoria Falls Hotel at the famous falls, and Leopard Rock in the Bvumba. There are many others that fall into the same bracket.

Note: Visitors are sometimes required to pay a higher rate for hotels than the locals, and usually in a non-Zimbabwean currency.

Accommodation in the wildlife and wilderness areas does not generally carry so many stars, but is usually more attractive and relaxing. The **National Parks accommodation** has to be booked well in advance (although one night is often possible on arrival), but most sought-after in areas such as Victoria Falls, Hwange, Kariba (Matusadona shore), Mana Pools, the Zambezi, Nyanga, Gonarezhou and the Matobo National Park are National Parks' fully equipped, self-catering chalets, tel: (14) 726089.

There are many **luxury safari lodges** throughout the country, usually in or near wildlife areas; all are highly recommended. The following organizations will suggest alternatives: Garth Thompson Safari Consultants, tel: (14) 795202; Shearwater Adventures, tel: (14) 735712; Safari Par Excellence, tel: (14) 720527; Phileas Fogg Travel, tel: (14) 704141 and Top of the Range, tel: (14) 738442.

Farm Holiday Association (including Ranch Safari Resorts) has a long list of country accommodation offering wildlife, tel: (14) 703978. Publicity associations in the various towns will supply more information. The magazine *Zimbabwe Travel News* publishes a regularly updated list, tel: (14) 725125.

Large wildlife conservancies in the Lowveld have changed from cattle to wildlife, turning rather to tourism, and are also offering safari accommodation. Phones are still uncertain but try Save Conservancy on fax: (131) 3097, Bubyana Conservancy on fax: (19) 60956, Chiredzi Conservancy on fax: (133) 6363.

PUBLIC HOLIDAYS

There are 13 annual holidays:
New Year's Day (January 1)
Good Friday to Easter Monday (4 days)
Independence Day (April 18)
Workers Day (May 1/2)
Africa Day (May 25)
Christmas Day (25 December)
Boxing Day (26 December)
Heroes Defence Force Days (August 11/12).

Trading Hours
Normal weekly hours are 08:30 to 17:00, and on Saturdays 08:30 to 13:00. Fairly widespread are supermarkets that stay open late on Sundays, as well as all-hours and small café trading.

Shopping
At the time of writing, all commodities (excluding unprocessed foods) carry an 14% general sales tax surcharge; the quoted price is inclusive of sales tax.

Measurements
Zimbabwe uses the metric system.

Telephones
The telecommunication system has been bad in the past, but is presently undergoing a major overhaul. STD dialling is possible to anywhere in the world on a usually fully automated system (dial 110 to obtain the international satellite, then 44 for the UK, 1 for the USA and Canada, 27 for South Africa and 61 for Australia).

In Zimbabwe, every exchange has its own dialling code. Where dashes occur in this code, it is an indication that you should wait for a second dialling tone before you dial the main number. To obtain operator assistance for local calls, dial O.

There are public phones in most of the main centres. Two phone books are printed: one for Harare, the other for the rest of the country. Facsimile (fax) facilities are also widely available.

Time
Zimbabwe is two hours ahead of Greenwich Mean (or Universal Standard) Time, one hour ahead of European Winter Time and seven hours ahead of the USA's Eastern Standard Winter Time. Sydney is eight hours ahead of Zimbabwe.

Electricity
The power system is 220 volts AC; US appliances require an adaptor. Plugs are usually 13-amp square pins.

Water
Tap water is safe to drink; keep away from river and dam water, which is often bilharzia-infected.

Medical Services
Pharmacies sell all necessary medicines. There is a list of medical doctors at the front of each town's phone entries in the telephone directory. Public hospitals are well equipped and there are many rural clinics; however, visitors should take out their own medical insurance. In an emergency one can go direct to the Casualty Department of a General Hospital. Hospitals are listed under 'Health' after city entry phone numbers in the directory. To contact the private medical air rescue service, tel: (14) 734513, or (Bulawayo) tel: (19) 64082.

Health Hazards
Sun: Sunburn can lead to skin cancer; use a minimum factor 15 (preferably paba-free) cream, and always wear a hat. Remember, a T-shirt is seldom sufficient protection against the sun's searing rays.
Malaria: Prophylactic treatment should be taken when visiting any areas other than the main plateau towns and Nyanga in the Eastern Highlands. Note that some strains of malaria are becoming immune to chloroquine, so

check first with your pharmacist when buying prophylactics. You should also try and avoid being bitten by applying insect repellant on exposed skin areas, and making use of mosquito nets.
Bilharzia: This debilitating waterborne disease caused by a parasitical worm can easily be caught from swimming in dams, rivers and pools other than those in Nyanga; avoid.
AIDS: HIV is a major disease in Zimbabwe. All visitors will be aware that abstention is the only 100% guarantee of avoiding this disease.
Creepy crawlies: Pepper ticks in the grasslands of the Eastern Highlands can itch for a week; wear long trousers and brush off after hiking. Blister beetles can cause a nasty rash; apply Stingose or a similar product.

Zimbabwe has a bonanza of insects, but very few visitors get bitten or stung by the nasty ones. Snakes usually try to avoid humans, while scorpion and spider bites are hardly ever fatal. Shake out your shoes and clothes in the early morning when on safari.

The most poisonous spider venom is that of the flat spider that lives on the interior walls of houses, but it is harmless as it cannot bite!

Emergencies
Dial 99 and stipulate either Police, Fire or Ambulance. The Samaritan Service (suicide or just the need to talk) in Harare is on tel: (14) 722000, or Bulawayo, tel: (19) 65000.

Security
In Zimbabwe drugs other than *mbanje* (cannabis) are novelties, not a way of life. And guns are rare (except on hunting safaris). There is the occasional armed robbery, however; cars are a favourite target and BMWs fetch a high price in Zambia and Zaïre. There is petty theft and pickpocketing. Backpackers should be wary of their valuables at camping sites, while putting forex under your mattress in a hotel is asking for trouble. Expensive clothes and running shoes (Adidas, Nike) are a magnet. Ignore black market forex touts; you can get a better deal in a bank.

CONVERSION CHART		
FROM	**TO**	**MULTIPLY BY**
Millimetres	inches	0.0394
Metres	yards	1.0936
Metres	feet	3.281
Kilometres	miles	0.6214
Hectares	acres	2.471
Litres	pints	1.760
Kilograms	pounds	2.205
Tonnes	tons	0.984
To convert Celsius to Fahrenheit: x 9 ÷ 5 + 32		

INDEX